pg. 63 - earn it.

pg. 90 - Know yourself.

pg. 113 - Focus on the response.

pg. 117 - Poise under pressure

pg. 118 - withstand the discomfort. — flooding.

pg. 121 - Control what you can - words and actions.
        ↳ body language.

pg. 122 - self-talk.

"A must-read for any athlete who has experienced tough losses, sidelining injuries, or major setbacks in their athletic journey. Packed with powerful lessons, this book will teach you how to do the little things right so that you can do the big things right when it matters."

Chris Hanson, 2x US squash national champion, RIA eyewear founder

"In today's world, sports have become so complicated, so layered . . . so hard. If you feel like the love of the game is slipping away from you, your child, or your athletes, this book is packed full of relatable stories, practical lessons, and expert insights you'll be referencing again and again."

Dr. Katherine Fairhurst, PhD, NCC, ACSM-CPT

"Julia Allain avoids traditional 'coach speak' with simple but appropriate messaging, exceptional storytelling, and clear lessons about teams and leadership. *Everything I Got* is a deep dive into the real value of sports and how individuals and teams can reach their full potential."

Andrew Copelan, 2021 PLL coach of the year, 2022 PLL champion

"The principles set out in this book redefine personal success and transcend sport to light a path for life beyond the athletic field. Anyone who seeks to confidently apply the same principles that drive world-class athletes into their lives will find accessible and achievable tools in these pages."

John Hayden, USA Hockey NTDP alum, NHL player

EVERYTHING I GOT

By Julia Allain

ISBN 13: 978-1-63489-581-1

Library of Congress Catalog Number has been applied for.
Printed in the United States of America
First Printing: 2023
27   26   25   24   23   5   4   3   2   1

Cover design by David Drummond
Interior design by Vivian Steckline

Wise Ink Creative Publishing
807 Broadway St. NE, Suite 46
Minneapolis, MN 55413
wiseink.com

To Mom, Dad, Josefine, and Nik, the best team anyone could have.

Contents

Introduction	**7**
1. Take Notes	**9**

Part One: IDENTITY

2. You Make the Player, the Player Doesn't Make You	**21**
3. Passion Builds from Purpose	**29**
4. Play for Three Things: for Fun, for Yourself and for Those Next to You	**34**
5. Things Happen—the Only Thing You Can Do Is the Next One	**43**
6. There Is No Such Thing as a Small Impact	**53**
7. Give Everything You Got Whatever That May Be	**59**
8. Your Pride Comes from Your Process	**67**
9. Where You Are Doesn't Change What You Do	**72**
10. To Do It Well First You Have to Have the Courage to Do It at All	**77**
11. There Is a Difference between Listening and Hearing	**83**
12. Your Greatest Resource Will Always Be Yourself	**88**

Part Two: EMOTIONS

13. Emotions Are Essential	**97**
14. Like a Muscle the Brain Needs Time to Develop Too	**104**
15. Don't Fight the Current	**112**
16. Talk the Talk	**119**

17. Look for What You Want   129

18. Be the Calm in the Storm
    Be the Storm in the Calm   135

19. Be Positive but Honest   142

20. Don't Worry About Them—Focus on You   149

21. The Past Doesn't Predict the Future   158

Part Three: GOALS

22. You Don't Have to Be the Best
    You Just Have to Be Your Best   169

23. Embrace Failure   174

24. Shoot for the Moon but Don't
    Lose Your Head in the Clouds   182

25. Our Greatest Reward Is Our Experience   189

26. Don't Be Afraid to Do Things Differently
    if You Want Different Results   196

27. Laugh Every Day   203

28. Create Your Own Momentum   212

29. Choose Your Team Wisely   220

THE FINAL LESSON

30. Sports Aren't Everything   228

Notes   233

Acknowledgments   243

About the Author   245

Introduction

The first time I ever met my dad was in Albany, New York. I was born just outside of Stockholm, Sweden, but that year the USA men's hockey team was training together in preparation for the 1992 Winter Olympics. My dad was one of the assistant coaches, and the team gave him a week off to travel to Sweden on my due date, but I never came. It is not like a coach's kid to be late for anything, and that was the last time I made that mistake: practice, appointments, airports, school, and meetings in general for the rest of my life—early was on time.

So, there I was, just about a month old, hanging out in a hotel room decorated by the USA men's hockey team with welcome signs, and that became my baseline for normal: Olympians, coaches, hotels, travel, sporting events, and family. It gave me the lens through which I viewed the world and gave me a world where I learned about life, a perspective filled with lessons that I put into this book.

Twenty-four years after that first meeting with my dad, I drove down from Montreal, where I was living at the time, and met him at the very same hotel in Albany. He was there with a hockey team again, this time preparing for the NCAA tournament. As he greeted me with excitement in the hotel parking lot, he asked me if the place looked familiar. While I had no recollection of the hotel itself beyond photographs in a family album, it amazed me how so much had changed in that twenty-four-year span of time, but also how much hadn't.

That second time, I got there early, and I had a bit more insight into this coaching thing my dad was doing. Not only was I in the process of earning a master's degree in sport psychology, but I had twenty-four years of watching games, engaging in conversations, and browsing the books and notebooks stacked on the shelves of our homes. The notebooks were filled with X's and O's, but also key words, quotes, and glimpses into the coaching philosophy of my dad and others he worked with. The books had worn-out bindings, highlighted sections, and notes in the margins.

Lesson 1

TAKE NOTES

My informal research as a curious kid browsing the resources scattered throughout my world led me to more formal research in graduate school. Studying coaches and athletic performance evolved from just a personal interest to a viable academic pursuit. After graduate school, I took my notes from school and life, all my resources and insight, and applied them as a teacher and coach myself. The professional experience offered new insight that school could not have provided me. As my career evolved and I expanded my experiential research with new positions and ventures, including starting my own performance consulting business at the age of twenty-six, the notes I was taking were piling up. While I stumbled through adversity, raced toward achievements, and battled through everything in between, I found the lessons I was learning about performance on the field were helping me navigate things not only as an athlete or coach but as a person as well. Slowly, I was developing a philosophy for life from experiences in a game.

On the field, I spent most of my time watching, playing, and coaching. Off the field, I continued to learn through reading, listening, and reflecting. The notes I have taken are from things I have read, people I have interacted with, and experiences I have had. I never kept a formal diary, but I filled pages with thoughts and ideas. I wrote down anything

I heard that resonated with me that I wanted to remember, reference, and use in my own life. Sometimes it was just a word or two; other times it was paragraphs. Over time, my own bookshelves became crammed with blank pages I had filled as a student of the game and of life. I wouldn't even throw out notebooks from college, in case I needed to reference those lectures one day—which I have, many times.

You can find my notes everywhere. Sometimes they are on my fridge, scattered on my desk, written on sticky notes attached to my computer, or scribbled along the pages of my daily planner. While it has been more than ten years since I played competitively, if you were to dig my old soccer bag out of my closet, you would find a folded-up piece of paper in the small front pocket. The red and blue ink from the lines had started to bleed a bit the last time I saw it, and I didn't have to unfold the paper to know what the words on the inside said. But I kept it there—a simple note as a reminder of how I wanted to play.

Since that first meeting in Albany, my notes have evolved from reflections on my personal experiences as an athlete, to research as a graduate student, to insight from my own coaching and teaching experiences. They have also moved beyond handwritten notes to digital ones. The photo album in my phone has become filled with screenshots and pictures of things I couldn't physically highlight but wanted to keep. Both my phone and Google frequently remind me of my storage limits, which I am constantly reaching before I can transfer my notes to another device.

In today's world, we don't always feel the need to write things down. With information so accessible to us, we allow things to come and go with the assumption that they will always be there for us to find again should we need them. The coaches and athletes who achieve greatness, however, stay true to their pen and paper: practices scribbled down in a hieroglyphic of *X*'s, *O*'s, and dotted lines; game notes taken on the bench; reflections written after a performance; and goals inked down and referenced. (In fact, as I was digging through my old notes in the process of writing this book, I came across a list of goals I had written in high school. Number one on the list was to write a book.) In graduate school, as I conducted research and interviewed elite coaches, every single one arrived at our meeting with notes to reference from the specific games we were about to discuss—often handing me my very own copy. In my role as a mental skills coach, I have observed that every athlete who has arrived at our meetings with a notebook and pen has gained ten times more than the ones who haven't, as evidenced by their progress throughout the years.

This book aspires to be one of those on the shelf with a worn-out binding, highlighted sections, and notes in the margins. As you read through this book, I hope you take notes. I hope you revisit the parts that mean the most to you, and I hope you question the things that you may disagree with. These lessons are meant to be implemented, but more importantly, they are meant to increase your self-awareness, make you think, and help you reach your full potential both on and off the field.

Part One

IDENTITY

" *I think that's what scared me the most when I quit. It wasn't losing the status of being an elite athlete or losing respect from those who undoubtedly would question my decision—I was scared to lose myself and to lose my place in the world. I was scared of no longer having that feeling that I belonged somewhere. It wasn't a social status to me, but an identity. If I hung up the cleats and threw out the jersey, what was left?* "

66 I really hate that Jágr."

Three-year-old me let out a big sigh for such a little person as I sat there eating my Cheerios on a nice July morning on Cape Cod. It was early, and my dad and I were eating breakfast together. My comment must have caught him off guard. So much so that he still recalls the moment and retells the story to this day, more than twenty-seven years later.

It was the summer of 1995, and Jaromír Jágr was on my mind. My dad was working for the Washington Capitals, and during the off-season, my family and I would go to Cape Cod, Massachusetts. Now, as hockey fans may know, the Washington Capitals and the Pittsburgh Penguins have had a pretty tumultuous relationship that really took off in the early 1990s due to their frequent meetings in the play-offs. In fact, the Penguins had so graciously given us our farewell party sending us on our way to the Cape that year. Thanks to the Penguins and their little-known star, Jaromír Jágr, summer came sooner than we had hoped in the Allain household.

I laugh whenever my dad tells this story because while I don't remember this exact moment, I really did hate him, and that I do remember. His name alone still evokes an aversive reaction in me to this day. Of course, I am now more able to appreciate and admire Jágr's career and what he has done within the sport of hockey, but that was not the case back then. To be honest, I wasn't even able to fully comprehend the intricate details of the game of hockey just yet at that age, so I hated him for his greasy, long hair that spilled out of his helmet as he flew across the ice. *Gross*, I thought.

But the reason for my hatred didn't matter so much as the result. My poor father, who thought he was so careful not to bring work home, had his three-year-old daughter ruminating over Jaromír Jágr in the middle of her summer morning breakfast. I can imagine he couldn't help but agree as we both went on chewing our food in a Jágr-sized despair.

And maybe that's when it started, my infatuation with the game. Not just sports, but the underlying game. The intricate underpinnings of it all. The stuff behind the curtain. The things the fans don't always get to see. The personal identities, the family involvement, the aftermath of losses, the emotions and frustrations we try to hide and bury deep down so they don't come out until we are sitting at breakfast one day in the middle of summer vacation and can't help but face the facts—man, we really hate that Jágr.

I have grown up in the thick of it. Tangled up inside the game, I have seen sports from every angle—I am the athlete, I am the coach's daughter, I am the athlete's sister, I am the fan, I am now a coach myself. I can't separate my life or myself from the athletic identity I have formed, from the victories I have tasted, and, more importantly, from the losses I have experienced. While I used to think it was dangerous to be defined by such an unpredictable and uncontrollable aspect of my life, I no longer believe that to be true. This game has shaped me and built me. It has given me an identity, and it has triggered and sparked more emotions in me than anything else, but more importantly, it has provided me with experience and perspective.

It started with my father's job, which gave me an inside look at the highs and lows of sports, and I have yet to find another roller coaster that I find more intoxicating. So I, too, threw myself into the fire. I put on the jersey; I dreamed of the trophies; I talked about it with my family at breakfast, lunch, and dinner. Soccer was my main sport; I put posters of soccer players on my ceiling so when I went to bed at night, I literally was looking at soccer stars. I won tournaments; I had shirts that said "champions"; I scored the winning goal in our high school conference final; I even went to a Division I school. Then I quit.

I *was* a soccer player. That took some time to get used to . . . *was*—past tense. You know, the tense they use when they describe someone in their obituary because they no longer exist. *I am a soccer player*, a sentence that I had identified with for so long, was no longer accurate. That version of me no longer existed. In one meeting, I said one sentence, and those words like a bullet transformed who I am into who I was. At first, I was ashamed and hated myself for my decision. I felt like I was letting down that little girl who spent her summer mornings still digesting the sudden and heartbreaking end of a season. I didn't face a Jágr who ended my playoff run or crushed my dreams. I walked away all on my own, and that became my identity. Maybe other people didn't define my identity based on that one decision, but deep down inside of me, quitting consumed who I thought I was the same way playing soccer and being an athlete used to consume my perception of myself.

As a result, I thought I should distance myself from the sport, and for a while I questioned the importance of these games. However, while I tried to eliminate any trace of sports from my identity, it proved to be impossible. It was too ingrained inside of me. It wasn't just one season or one team that made me, but a lifetime of games. A lifetime of wins and losses, of celebrations and heartbreaks. While I did my best to avoid wearing any attire associated with my college team and quickly tried to correct anyone who misidentified me as a soccer player, I couldn't erase the experiences that I had already had. It wasn't that soccer and sports in general defined me as a person, but they were things that molded and shaped me.

The impact was everlasting, even if the game itself was not.

Oftentimes, professional athletes, or aspiring professional athletes, will say they are married to the game. It is an analogy that reveals many truths about sports at that level. It requires commitment, patience, compromise, work, and a lot of ups and downs. But most importantly, you have a love for the game the same way people have love for their families. You may fight with it, it can disappoint you, and you will complain about it constantly, but you would do anything for it. No questions asked.

Like any good marriage, the game should also include laughter and a whole lot of joy. It should bring out the best in you and make you a better and happier person. However, the challenge with marriage, and with sports, is that oftentimes we become so consumed with the role or title, of being the soccer player or being a spouse, that we lose ourselves in that process. We not only sacrifice who we are in order to fulfill the role, which is only a portion of our whole selves, but begin to define and value ourselves based on that role. Am I a good spouse? Am I a good soccer player? If the marriage fails, or if my team fails, then I, too, am a failure. Hyper-focused on the product or outcome, we no longer pay attention to the important process those roles require.

But in reality, the best marriages aren't just about the marriage itself. They highlight the best attributes in people and allow them to continue to grow both in and outside of the union. Sports offer the same. The value isn't whether you are a good player or not, but in the attributes the game highlights in you and the growth opportunities it provides. When it is all said and done, whether you win the championship or get divorced, if you walk away from it all changed for the better—stronger, smarter, and more self-aware—then it becomes a valuable process of growth, contributing to who you become, but not a final statement about who you are.

I didn't always understand this, and in the same way a person may continually analyze a failed relationship or a bad breakup, I was kept up at night trying to figure out where it all went wrong. Years later, I would still dream about the one that got away, the one I should have fought harder for. Filled with thoughts of what we could have and should have been, I frequently missed the feeling I got on that field. A feeling of ecstasy and happiness, but more importantly a feeling of comfort. The way some may feel like they fit perfectly in the arms of their first love, I felt safe between those lines on the field. Especially as a teenager, during a time in our lives when we so often feel lost and confused, I felt a sense of belonging because of the sports in my life. I had a team. I had a goal . . .

I had a passion that I mistook as an identity.

But as life continued on, whether I was playing soccer or not, what I began to gain was perspective that only time and maturity could provide me. This perspective included appreciation for the sport and the lessons I learned, but more importantly appreciation for myself and the person I realized I was with or without a ball at my feet. What I realized was that I didn't lose a part of myself when I walked away from the sport, but instead I had always put a part of myself into the game.

I think that's what scared me the most when I quit. It wasn't losing the status of being an elite athlete or losing respect from those who undoubtedly would question my decision—I was scared to lose myself and to lose my place in the world. I was scared of no longer having that feeling that I belonged somewhere. It wasn't a social status to me, but an identity. If I hung up the cleats and threw out the jersey, what was left?

Lesson 2

YOU MAKE THE PLAYER
THE PLAYER DOESN'T
MAKE YOU

What I've learned since then is that it wasn't the soccer that made me, it was the parts of me that made the player I was. I wasn't the fastest or most skilled, but I was composed, and I was competitive. Each decision, although not always successful, was calculative. I was purposeful, but I was also goofy. I laughed more than I cried on that field. I joked more than I yelled. I still am all of those things, even off the field. Those are still things that go into the work I do, regardless of what that work is: the products I create, the relationships I build, the successes I have, and, more importantly, the failures I have.

The danger in thinking that the player makes you is not only that it limits who you are and what you can become outside of the sport, but that it limits your success in the game as well. Tying your identity too closely to your performance makes the performance stressful rather than enjoyable. It causes the sport to drain everything out of you rather than motivate you. I've seen this when players start to devalue themselves based on negative sport outcomes and begin pushing themselves out of fear that they are a lesser person if they don't succeed rather than out of passion for the game itself.

But fear isn't fuel; it is fire.

Fear can eventually burn so hot that you burn out. Enjoyment, on the other hand, fills you up. It makes the challenges and obstacles seem smaller, the outcomes seem brighter, and the overall experience seem easier because it is fun. As a result, you will not only be able to go further for longer, but will also improve and learn more along the way.

When I first started as a mental skills coach, I spent time with athletes deconstructing their identities, so their sport wasn't prioritized at the top. Sports are what you do, what you love, not who you are. However, as time has gone on, I have shifted my approach a bit. Why can't we prioritize the thing that has taught us so much about ourselves and about life? The issue arises not when we tie our identity closely to our sport but when we value our identity based on our sport outcomes. As former number-one golfer in the world, Rory McIlroy, has been quoted saying on numerous occasions, "I am not my score. I am not my results."

You as an athlete and your performance outcomes are two very different things. Who you are as a player matters, and it is allowed to matter. What you achieve as a player doesn't matter because it doesn't change who you are. In fact, the value of this critical difference was demonstrated in a study that examined athlete burnout.[1] Athlete burnout is a common challenge among high-performing athletes who have dedicated extreme amounts of time and energy to their sport. It is a mixture of both physical and emotional exhaustion that leads to a reduction in motivation and thus performance outcomes. The research found that having a strong identity that is tied to sport did not lead to that dangerous burnout in athletes; instead, it provided resistance to it. Not only was the athletic identity not detrimental for the athlete, as many people thought, but it was beneficial. Those at risk for burnout were the athletes who based their self-confidence and self-worth on their accomplishments.

Playing a sport and being an athlete are ingrained in our identities, and it would be foolish of us to try to ignore that. It clearly provides strength and purpose that allow us to persevere when our self-esteem may cause us to waver. More importantly, having a clear, strong identity can help you become a better athlete. While some people may mistakenly try to change themselves to live up to a certain ideal, you don't have to change who you are to become the ideal player because the ideal player requires you to become the best version of yourself. The ideal player isn't one set of specific guidelines or traits, but rather someone who brings their full self to the game, utilizes all their strengths, and wants to improve their weaknesses. That is what makes you irreplaceable as an athlete. At a certain level, everyone will be skilled, everyone will be dedicated and hardworking, but no one else will be you.

One of the best examples of this and one of the most unique personalities in professional sports was NBA player Dennis Rodman. He brought things to his role and position that no one else could bring. He without a doubt made the player, and the type of player he became was incomparable to anyone else. Even Rodman himself said that he didn't fit the mold of a typical NBA player. He dyed his hair different colors, wore eccentric outfits, and lived a lifestyle that was questioned by many people associated with the game. But he brought those same qualities to the court. He was a player who pushed boundaries and tested people. Rodman wasn't afraid to get hurt, piss people off, or disrupt everyone else's game plan. He was in your face, and as a result he got in a lot of people's heads. He wasn't always the easiest to work with, and his teammates and coaches had their work cut out for them in efforts to manage him effectively, but he was even tougher to play against.

Playing alongside other legends such as Michael Jordan, Rodman was smart enough to realize that his job wasn't to aspire to be another Michael Jordan or to emulate anyone else. His job was to play his role the way only he could. In the documentary series *The Last Dance*, Rodman was quoted as saying, "You got the great Michael Jordan, the great Scottie Pippen, the great Phil Jackson. But if you take me away from this team, do they still win a championship? I don't think so. I love Michael Jordan to death. I love Scottie Pippen, all these guys. But they really don't do the things that I do." While Rodman may have faced a lot of critics throughout his career, he was fortunate enough to find teammates and coaches who knew who he was, saw his value, and pushed him to not change but to become the best version of himself that they knew he could be: a version that helped them all find historic levels of success.

When you bring your best to the game and define the type of player you want to be rather than allowing the game to define you as a person, then you can't lose yourself in the sport. You may find your strength, your passion, and even your purpose inside the confines of the game, but you can't get lost in it.

Because regardless of the result, win or lose, success or failure, you are still you.

That can never be taken from you. And the things you can gain are found more often through the failures than any of the successes.

In 2012, about a year and a half after I quit soccer, I

remember watching as Nastia Liukin competed in the Olympic trials for gymnastics in preparation for the Summer Games in London. She was competing for a spot on the team that would represent the USA at the Olympics. However, Nastia wasn't just an Olympic hopeful like everyone else competing that day. She had won five medals at the Beijing Olympic Games just four years earlier, including gold as the all-around champion. This meant that she was the best gymnast in the world and trying to defend her title. If she performed well at these trials and made the Olympic team again, she would be the first American female gymnast in twelve years to compete in back-to-back Olympics. If she didn't make the team, then her career would be over.

At those trials in 2012, four years after her dreamlike experience in China, Nastia found herself lying face first on the mat just below the uneven bars, arguably her best event. It was one of those moments where even as a spectator you could feel the wind get knocked out of you as her hands missed the bars in midair and she hit the mat, her body completely parallel to the floor. Then Nastia got back up and finished her routine. While all of her successes in gymnastics are more than impressive, it was her career-ending failure that day that I find even more inspiring.

Still in college at the time, still struggling with my own post-athletic identity, I was heartbroken for her and her epic failure. She wasn't going to make the Olympic team, and her career was over. However, years later, I listened to Nastia retell her own account of that moment on the Just Women's Sports podcast *The Players' Pod* with Kelley O'Hara, USA women's national soccer team player. In the conversation, she shared how she came to her own realization in that very moment that she was more than just her performance, and, more importantly, that other people valued her beyond her identity as a gymnast.

"All of a sudden," Nastia explained, "I started seeing people stand on their feet. And I was like 'That must be nice, someone else just went and had the best routine of their life and they are on their way to making the Olympic team . . .' I quickly realized these people were giving me a standing ovation. It was the first standing ovation of my entire career for the worst routine of my entire career. And that was the moment that I realized we are not defined by our success. We are not defined by a placement, a medal, a title, a salary, a job title, a relationship. Any of those things don't define us as people."

Listening to her talk, I could relate to Nastia in a way I never imagined I would when I watched her at the Olympics years earlier. Despite my own struggles to come to terms with my perceived failure when I quit, those around me never wavered in their love or support. So many people assumed because of my life leading up to that moment my decision was more dramatic. "But what do your parents think? What does your dad think?" they would all ask. Having grown up in such a sports-oriented environment, these sports surely must mean more to us. We must value it more. You could ask my dad, but I'm pretty sure he hasn't disowned me yet. I'm his daughter. I play soccer. The first statement doesn't change because the second one does. None of it defined who I was as a person, especially not to the people around me. When I quit, when I thought of myself as a failure, they gave me a hug. There was no look of disappointment or letdown. There was only love and endless support.

People may have been surprised by my family's reaction, but I wasn't. Since I was born, I had been watching the people involved with sports at the highest level. While that experience surrounds you with people achieving their ultimate goals, it provides you with the realization that many people don't achieve those dreams. You see the losses that are all more common than the victories. More importantly, I saw the person who was behind each athlete. I saw the players take their helmets off and reveal their scarred and bruised faces, saw the coaches loosen their ties, and saw them all hug their family members after every tough loss or nail-biting win. It didn't matter the outcome or the score because those scars, those hugs, and all those postgame gatherings always held a great deal of honor, pride, and love.

Those experiences are things that bonded people faster and stronger than anything else I have come across in my life. They form relationships that can span across years and continents, time and space. They are holidays spent together, whether at a house or a hotel. The value never resides in the medals or the outcomes.

It exists in the experience itself.

The goosebumps you feel when the anthem plays, the racing hearts as the clock counts down, and the teary eyes at the end of the season. It includes all the late nights and struggles leading up to that moment: the goals against, the grueling workouts, the mistakes, the injuries, and the disappointments. The postgame gatherings in my family's living room until well past midnight where we all agree that we need to go to bed, but all have too much adrenaline to fall asleep.

My perceived failure as a quitter almost drove me away from sports. But I couldn't walk away that easily. Instead, my journey off the field became more about the game than ever before. It drove me to research, it drove me to learn, and it drove me right back into the game that I initially thought I should distance myself from. Suddenly, I found myself sitting in the front seat of the intoxicating roller-coaster ride of sports again. However, this time I was not focused on my identity as an athlete but rather trying to better understand myself and others, better manage situations, and eventually better impact those who followed behind me—those who became as infatuated with the game as I did.

Lesson 3

PASSION BUILDS
FROM PURPOSE

Since the beginning, I was a soccer player. That's what I always was. I don't have memories of the first time I kicked a ball or put on a pair of cleats. There is no moment where I fell in love with the game. In fact, it wasn't ever something I fell in love with. It was simply what I felt like I became. My knees were forever bruised, I wore my team gear all the time, and my hair was always in a ponytail. In fifth grade, while the girls played four square at recess, I played soccer with the boys. When everyone got new L. L. Bean backpacks in the fall with their initials, I got a new Nike backpack with my number. In high school, I had more sneakers than high heels and more team hoodies than dresses. It wasn't a conscious choice I made to be the athletic girl; it was the only thing that ever felt like it fit, until it didn't anymore.

Like trying to place a twin-size sheet on a king-size bed, suddenly things weren't lining up. Something was missing, and I no longer felt like myself in the game. Was it me or the game that changed? I always knew that I was never playing for a scholarship or a title. I never cared about the name of the team I was on. I cared about winning because I am competitive and winning is fun, but I cared about playing well even more. This I know is true, because I cried after victories when I didn't enjoy the quality of the game more than I cried after losing. Most of all, I cared about everything it gave me. Soccer gave me joy. It gave me a sense of belonging. It gave me goals to chase after. It gave me all the lessons in this book. That's why I played, and when those things were suddenly hard to find, it didn't feel right anymore.

Motivation, even as a child, was always a topic of intrigue for me. A coach is always trying to motivate others, and being the daughter of a coach, I was able to be a bystander in many discussions trying my best to figure out how to motivate. I'd sympathetically listen as my father tried to formulate a plan to motivate his players, maybe even offer advice if I ever had any. Some of the best advice, however, probably came from my sister in 2009, a few years after my dad started coaching at Yale University.

In the middle of a historic season for the Yale hockey team, where they were experiencing unprecedented success and, as a result, the pressure that comes along with it, my dad was looking to keep his players motivated and driven. My sister suggested they leave the rink and go play some pond hockey. Go have fun and let loose. So, they took her advice; my dad and Wayne Dean, his associate athletic director, made some calls, checked the weather, and scheduled a date on the pond at the Yale golf course. In an article posted a few days later on the Yale Athletics website, senior Pat Brosnihan was quoted as saying, "We get caught up in the season and being so focused on winning.

 ## It's easy to forget why you love this game.

This slowed things down for us and helped us realize why we love it so much." Less than two months later, in March, they won the first ever Eastern College Athletic Conference title in Yale history.

"What's your why?" is a question I have asked and been asked numerous times since I have become a mental skills coach. It is the ultimate foundation for long-term sustained performance, in any context. It is your reason, your purpose—it is your motivation for doing whatever it is that you are doing. Is it for fortune and fame, or is it for fun and the love of the game? Is it for you, or are you doing this for someone else? If you know your why, you will be able to harness it and use it to push you forward and push you through the challenges you will inevitably face.

Research done in 2018, examining the impact of having a strong purpose on managing daily stress, demonstrated that knowing your reason for doing something can lead to greater overall well-being.[2] Specifically, the participants in the study who reported a higher sense of purpose in life also reported fewer negative emotions, such as feeling sad, worthless, nervous, irritable, or frustrated, and they reported greater positive emotions, such as feeling happy, peaceful, attentive, confident, and enthusiastic. In addition, they also reported fewer physical symptoms such as headaches and fatigue. These results suggest that having a strong sense of your "why" may better equip you to overcome obstacles and regulate emotions, not just in sports, but in your day-to-day life.

Years after I had quit soccer, my mother was surprised when she heard me sharing my story. She was taken aback by the fact that I used the term *quit* when referring to the end of my athletic career. She told me I made it sound so sudden, like I gave up in the middle of a game or a season. I shrugged and said that I had three years left of college—it was in the middle of it. With a confused look on her face, she told me she never saw it like I quit. She said I walked away when the experience wasn't fulfilling anymore. I had too much love and respect for the game and myself, and I wouldn't let that be destroyed by staying in a situation that was no longer any fun.

Quitting has a bad reputation. It is seen as something reserved for losers, the weak, and simply those who can't cut it. Quotes from great athletes and coaches replay in every young athlete's head when they think about stopping, echoing the same sentiment: "Winners never quit. Quitters never win." They emphasize the ultimate goal of victory, and the ultimate sin of quitting.

There is valuable truth in that statement. We shouldn't turn our backs when things get difficult. Greatness requires us to push ourselves a little bit further and a little bit harder than ever before. It does not just fall into our laps easily. However, quitting and success are not mutually exclusive. When you walk away, you give up the potential that exists in that moment; however, you may also gain new possibilities.

Would you stay at a stable job in corporate America where you make a good salary even if you are unhappy? That may depend on your reasons for working, but the Murray brothers, Shep and Ian, didn't. They both quit their New York City jobs within ten minutes of each other back in 1998. They then maxed out their credit cards and sold neckties out of the trunk of their car. Their new passion became the clothing company Vineyard Vines, which is valued at more than a billion dollars today.

In an article on Business Insider, Ian, the younger brother, was quoted as saying, "Quality of life was more important to us than financial gain."[3] However, there is no need to sacrifice one for the other, as by prioritizing their quality of life, the brothers managed to also profit financially.

Too often, we think there is only one way to find and define success, when in reality there are many different versions of success that exist and ways to get there.

Shep followed up his brother's quote by saying, "I think a lot of people measure success financially. If you do that, it doesn't necessarily always lead to a happier, more productive life. Make sure you do things for the right reasons."

The most important reason for my family and me when it came to dedicating so much time to sports was always the experience. Not the money or the trophies but the enjoyment and fulfillment that came from the process itself. With so much sacrifice, we knew that if it wasn't fun anymore, then the cost wouldn't be worth it. While our lives had given us an understanding as to why people are willing to give up so much and battle through physical and mental pain for a simple game, we also understood when it comes to an end.

Wherever you are in life, and whatever you are doing, take time to reflect on your reasons and purpose. What is it that motivates you, where is it you want to be, and, most importantly, why do you want those things? Write them down, keep them close, and remind yourself of them when you need an extra push or some clarity. Revisit them, and don't be afraid to revise them. As you grow and your life evolves, those reasons may change, and that is OK. However, if you are unsure of where to begin or what your reasons are, that's OK too. There are some reasons that we can all fall back on when struggling to find our why.

Lesson 4

PLAY FOR THREE THINGS:
FOR FUN
FOR YOURSELF
AND FOR THOSE NEXT TO YOU

Some people may question why athletes sacrifice so much for sports, but an athlete's motivation was never something I questioned. It was just what you did. It was a feeling that I understood but always found difficult to put into words. Unless you have been a part of it, you may never truly understand the power of that driving force behind the hours of practice, preparation, and even pain that sports require.

For me, those things were always worth it in the beginning. However, soon into my high school career, I started to see the process get tainted with a focus on performance outcomes and external rewards, things that we know contribute to burnout and demotivation. These rewards, like college scholarships, occupied everyone's minds—parents, teammates, and even coaches. It wasn't until all this started happening that I began to realize a lot of people dedicated all this time and money into sports as an investment for the future. There was an exchange where they expected something tangible in return. They pay now, in time, money, and work, so hopefully the sport will pay back later in the form of college tuition or, better yet, a professional contract. It is shocking looking back on how I grew up around sports as a career, but it never dawned on me to play for something other than for fun up until that point.

At first, it was small things like my teammates starting to get paid by their parents for every goal they scored. Five dollars each time the ball found the back of the net. I thought it was weird, and honestly pretty stupid, but what I thought was the most ironic part of all was that it didn't actually help them perform any better. This motivation just gave them tunnel vision. Focused solely on their own results and stats, my teammates who were getting paid overlooked the pass or better play in order to try and score so they could get their money. To them, one goal they scored was more valuable than three goals our team scored together, which limited our overall success.

Unfortunately, this shift in mindset not only impacted the quality of our playing but also took many people away from the key things that provide an athlete with consistent and resilient motivation. Although the actual feelings an athlete gets when they are driven and committed in a sport may be difficult to describe or understand, the factors behind them, I think, are pretty simplistic. First and foremost, fun, while not always prioritized as the primary motivating factor behind many athletes' drive, is the most important.

If you want long-term, sustained motivation and performance, fun is a nonnegotiable element of the process.

Without any enjoyment, the sacrifices and work will wear you down until you have nothing left in the tank. If you are enjoying yourself, you not only are more likely to be present in the moment, but you also won't be as distracted by the challenges associated with your performance, such as the pressure, the pain, or even the failures along the way. Suddenly you will feel fortunate for the experience, rather than dwelling on the cost of the extreme sacrifice.

Sometimes people might forget, but having fun is important even for the most serious competitors. In fact, it was one of the top three goals, right along with improving overall performance and winning, for Olympic athletes in a study that examined their goal-setting practices.[4] Even Jordan Spieth, another former world number-one golfer, aims to play with more fun as a part of his game. In an interview during the PGA Tour in 2020, he was asked about what he wished he knew about golf when he was younger. He thought for a moment and responded, "Honestly, I wish I played with the mentality I had back then now. You overthink the game the more you are out. You just want to play like a kid, just freewheel it and have fun . . . just don't take it too seriously. Because I didn't back then and the only times the game has been too difficult for me is when I did take it too seriously."[5]

If you are focused on having fun, then the second factor behind that motivation falls into place very easily—playing for yourself. You are on the field, the court, or the ice because you want to be there, not because someone else wants you there. It is a choice you get to make for yourself every day, and when you are having fun, it is an easy choice to make. But even when it challenges you, you choose to persevere. It isn't out of obligation, or responsibility, but for yourself and your own personal goals, growth, and desire.

Sports can simultaneously be the hardest and best part of your day when you prioritize yourself in the process.

Finally, those next to you are irreplaceable when it comes to motivation. Humans are naturally social creatures. We not only yearn for connection with others but have evolved with a natural instinct to work together in groups. This instinct is often reflected in our feelings of loneliness when we don't feel a part of the group. According to some theories, loneliness is triggered as a reminder that coming together, whether it be as a team, a tribe, or a family, provides mutual protection and assistance that helps us survive.[6] Like hunger motivates us to find food, loneliness motivates us to connect with a group.

As a result, we are psychologically drawn to these team environments because survival, both on any field and in life, is less likely when you are alone. When we become part of a team, we feel safer and more secure, but we also become a part of something much greater than ourselves. This motivates us to want to protect and preserve that unit more than anything. It is the same psychological effect of a team environment that has motivated humans throughout history to sacrifice for their family, to go to war, and to protect the group at all costs.

Abby Wambach, former USA national soccer team player, described the importance of the team in her book *Wolfpack*.[7] Having scored more international goals than any other man or woman in the history of the game when she retired, Abby is an incredible athlete all on her own. However, as she reveals in her book, what she loved the most about soccer wasn't her individual stats or her medals but being a part of a team. In her own words, Abby explains, "I loved winning and losing as ONE team. I loved being a part of something bigger than myself. I loved the shared joy, suffering, failure, and success. I loved the magic of collectively surrendering to an unknown outcome." Later in her book she explains the impact that the team had on her ability to push through challenges, something she didn't even notice until it was gone. Three years after her retirement, Wambach struggled to get back into a fitness routine with a simple daily running challenge. Shocked by the difficulty of running, which she assumed would be easy compared to her previous training regimes, she realized that without her team around her, both suffering alongside her and encouraging her along the way, the pain and difficulty of the task were amplified.

Life, especially training, was much harder alone.

For the most part, my life in sports lived up to this ideal focused on fun, myself, and my team. I have had more fun on the soccer field, in the hockey stands, and behind the bench than anywhere else in my life. I have had a lot of laughs, I have learned a lot of skills and lessons, and I have gained lifelong friends and family. As a result, no matter what happened, whether it was losing every game at a tournament or losing the league championship game in overtime, it was still worth it. Every heartbreak and disappointment. That is why when my college experience didn't go how I expected it to and didn't last nearly as long as it was meant to, I had no regrets about all the time I had spent dedicated to the game, because it was still worth it. And if I had the choice to go back and do my childhood again, I wouldn't spend a second less on that field or in those hours-long car rides going to practice. However, I didn't realize how important the joy was in all the traditional success I was able to have until after it faded away and was overcome by the frenzy and focus of a new goal—a goal centered on money and accolades.

For me, when that college recruiting process began to take priority across all aspects of my teams, from showcase tournaments to college informational sessions, I began to get frustrated with the politics of it all. Suddenly, the game off the field—who you talk to, how you sell yourself, and what money you could get—became more important than the game on the field. For a young kid in the moment, it can be overwhelming trying to balance all the different components of that process, and the opinions and expectations of those around you, while still playing for fun and yourself. While I was fortunate that my parents never bought into the drama, even when it felt like the rest of the world did, I wasn't blind to the effects on those around me.

In 2019, a national survey conducted by the Aspen Institute with the Utah State University Families in Sport Lab revealed the impact that this cultural change was having on youth sport participation overall.[8] Its results showed that the average kid in the United States quits the sport they are playing by the age of eleven, playing for a total of less than three years. This is a few years before many kids begin to enter puberty, where their bodies begin to grow and develop, and about seven years before an athlete would head off to college. Seven years of experiences, memories, and development they miss out on. From a performance standpoint, if we begin to eliminate our athletes at age eleven, then we limit our talent pool and potential at every level that follows: high school, college, professional, and even international.

The primary reason for their early departure from the sport? According to the survey, it just wasn't fun anymore. These results echoed another study completed in 2014 that found both lack of enjoyment of the sport and not feeling good enough were the two most dominant factors related to athletes dropping out.[9] Contributing to the lack of fun and negative self-evaluations was the financial investment now required to participate in many youth sports, which increased the pressure surrounding the young athletes. As Dr. Travis Dorsch, founding director of the Families in Sport

Lab, explained, "For the parent who's putting down $10,000 for their kid to play soccer, they see it as giving their kid every opportunity. But the kid may feel, 'Oh my gosh, they're putting down $10,000 and now I feel pressure to perform.'" Now that they're clearly no longer playing for themselves or for fun, their motivation and overall experience suffer.

While many of the parents have good intentions and want their kids to have fun playing sports, they can't deny the appeal of some of the extrinsic rewards that are possible. The Families in Sport Lab survey also assessed the reasons parents had for wanting their kids involved in sport on a scale of 1–5 (5 being most important). Results of the survey showed that fun ranked the highest, earning a score of 4.49. However, admission to college, athletic scholarships, and professional sports opportunities were close behind, all ranking above 3. These findings aren't just being given attention in research labs, as popular news sources are even taking time to report on the impact of the increasing pressure and demand being placed on young athletes.[10] One 2019 news article titled "Experts Cite 'Bully Parents' in Decline in Youth Sports Participation Nationwide" suggested that while parents claim to prioritize fun, many of their actions say otherwise. As the article claims, "Out-of-control behavior of some parents, both on the sidelines and in the home, is fostering a culture that emphasizes winning and perfectionism over physical activity and enjoyment—one that experts say is toxic for children."

Beyond simply threatening the level of participation in youth sports, this shift in priorities that has continued to add to the stress young athletes experience also takes away some of the true value of athletics. Rather than focusing on supporting and developing athletes and teaching them values such as teamwork, youth sports foster a cutthroat environment focused on superficial results that cultivate little team unity and even less enjoyment. Due to this shift in the mindset of youth sports from a game to a business, prioritizing money and external rewards, college athletics are being discussed even sooner than high school these days, a trend that I find terrifying and dangerous for the future of athletics and, more importantly, the athletes.

By causing young athletes to worry that something will be taken from them, like an opportunity, a scholarship, or simply a spot on a team, youth sports have fostered a fear-based motivation rather than gain-based motivation. Not embracing the things we can get from the experience, such as fun and valuable lessons and skills, athletics today emphasizes what you might lose, which is both exhausting and limiting. If we are focused too much on the fear and pressure of expectations, then the overall enjoyment that makes the difficult moments more bearable and the fun and laughter that the game is meant to provide are lost completely.

Working with so many young athletes today, it breaks my heart to see the stress and pressure they are experiencing at such early ages. The place that was an escape for me as a kid has turned into the main source of stress for others. High school and even middle school parents frequently reach out to me because they notice their children are experiencing extreme levels of performance anxiety. Then they spend a majority of our conversation talking about their children's potential and opportunities in the future for them within their sports, if only their kids could get it together. I patiently listen and then try to explain that their goals will be difficult to reach if their children are no longer having fun playing the game at the age of thirteen. While some athletes manage to get through the intense years of college recruitment, the longevity of their athletic experiences is still at risk. Their performance is not sustainable with so much weighing them down mentally and emotionally.

I saw this firsthand as I sat with a college athlete after a difficult week. He let out a huge sigh as he glanced out the window over to the rink where he spent most of his time training and competing. "All the athletic donors I met told me that is the rink that I built," he said, referring to the promise of his potential that had inspired the millions of dollars of donations to the athletic department. The eighteen-year-old didn't say it with pride, or excitement, or joy. He said it with a heavy sense of obligation, like a debt that he had to repay. This game had already become a job and, at that time, a burden to him.

When I was a college athlete, I watched as seniors on my team celebrated the last game of the season not because we won a championship but because the season was finally over and they (as seniors) were finally free. While I too was relieved that the season was complete, I felt confused and unsettled. Every year of my life, I had watched adult men crying after their last game because their season had ended. That was the experience I was expecting. Yet, the only tears I experienced that year were from frustration and disappointment. It was clear that many of us were not focused on playing for fun, for ourselves, or even for each other. We were just playing to get through it.

When you anchor your purpose to an outcome centered on a tangible goal or title, such as winning a championship or simply surviving to say you were a Division I athlete, you eliminate much of the value the experience can provide you. If you instead can play for those three key things—for fun, yourself, and those next to you—not only will you appreciate the opportunity you have more, but you will energize yourself with the motivation necessary to perform and persevere even through the most difficult challenges.

Lesson 5

THINGS HAPPEN
THE ONLY THING YOU
CAN DO IS THE NEXT ONE

We all know there will be many challenges that will continue to push us to improve and help us grow, both on and off the playing field. If we aren't playing for the right reasons, then the stakes and pressure can feel higher and those challenges or bumps in the road can rock us a bit more. However, no matter what, everyone is susceptible to the bumps along the way to reaching their goals. This journey never goes in the smooth, straight line that we hope or envision it will, and despite how hard we may try, we can't control everything.

Getting injured, getting fired or cut from a team, losing games from unlucky bounces or bad calls—things happen. Good things and bad things, happy and sad. While all our experiences are different, the adversity that comes with unexpected complications is one of the few universal experiences that even the best athletes in the world have to face at one point or another. When an athlete's plans are disrupted, it is then that their focus is truly tested. It is easy to stay motivated and on task when everything is going well and according to plan. It is much harder when nothing is going the way you expected or intended it to.

In an attempt to minimize the challenges that they will

undoubtedly face, high performers are naturally very structured individuals. They create routines, they stick to their plans, and they micromanage as much as they can. This can be as small and seemingly insignificant as the number of times a basketball player bounces the ball before taking a free throw or as big and time consuming as their detailed daily schedule leading up to competition.

Studies have shown that these simple routines have been found to help athletes feel more composed and perform better in high-pressure situations. In fact, one study examining the impact of routines on elite pistol shooters' performance found that routines not only improved the shooting scores of participants but also decreased the variance in their shooting, meaning that they were also shooting more consistently overall.[11] These routines included intentionally planned-out steps before shooting, such as specific breathing patterns, guided self-talk scripts, and actions detailing where to look and what to do.

While that study analyzed routines in the moment right before executing a skill, Sidney Crosby, one of the NHL's most prominent stars, has become well known for his carefully structured game day routine. In a 2010 episode of the documentary series *24/7*, which gives fans access to the day-to-day events of NHL teams, Crosby walked through his detailed pregame routine. It included a specific route from his car to the locker room, the process of taping his stick, the preparation of his peanut butter and jelly sandwich, his warm-up and stretching, and even the sequence of putting on his gear. "You're not going to have any trouble finding me at a certain time before a game," Crosby said, implying that the specific time he does each action is as equally controlled as the actions themselves. "It's the same every single game."

Crosby was a first-round draft pick of the Pittsburgh

Penguins in 2005, and since then, he has earned countless accolades. My dad was working at the draft that year and woke up early the first day to work out before heading over to the conference center. He recalls an empty gym at 6:00 a.m. in Ottawa that morning, except for one other person—a young but already disciplined Sidney Crosby. While everyone knew he would be the first overall pick that day, Crosby didn't take a day off from his preparation or workout routine. Since that morning, not much has changed in his consistent approach.

But even the most detail-oriented coaches and meticulous athletes aren't immune to obstacles along the way.

Their carefully constructed plans and routines are frequently derailed by the unpredictable consequences of the game, highlighting the instability of it all. Crosby, for instance, fell victim to the unpredictable detours the game threw at him, suffering major injuries and adversity throughout his career. Just two episodes after revealing his carefully controlled pregame routine, Crosby got hit in the head on the ice. While that hit did not sideline him, just a few days later, a second hit resulted in a concussion diagnosis that left him sidelined for the rest of the season and the start of the following one, unable to return to a game until the end of November the next season. His return, however, was short lived, as he reappeared on the injury list in December, missing the next forty games with continued concussion symptoms and a neck injury. In fact, multiple times throughout the following seasons, Crosby's plans were cut short or interrupted due to injuries and other unforeseen complications. As a result, he had to adjust his routines, and he had to shift his focus from controlling his preparation to responding to the situation.

While Crosby was the youngest NHL captain to win a Stanley Cup when he did so at twenty-one years old in 2009, all those injuries he eventually suffered contributed to some less-than-spectacular years for the record-breaking captain. In March 2016, *Sports Illustrated* ran a story titled "The Crosby Conundrum: Entering Middle Age, Who Is Sid the Kid?" criticizing the decrease in his production on the ice and questioning his value and ability to impact the game like he once seemed destined to do.[12] As Crosby discussed the tough stretch in his career, he didn't dwell on the moment or the injuries or the bad things that happened, but instead focused on getting better and moving forward. "I don't know for sure when I'm going to get out of this," Crosby said. "But when I do, I'll be all the stronger for it."

As the article went on, wondering what the future held for the humbled super star, Crosby didn't take the opportunity to feel sorry for himself or his situation. "Are you going to make excuses and give up or are you going to find ways to make yourself better for everyone else?" he asked himself rhetorically, highlighting an important lesson he'd learned through the adversity he was faced with. Things happen, but what could he do about it now? That was March 2016. In June of that year, after years of responding to adversity by staying committed and focusing on what he could do to get better and be ready for the next opportunity when it came, Crosby led the Penguins to another Stanley Cup championship. And then another one the year after that.

Those who achieve great results prepare not for simple and straightforward success without criticism or adversity. Rather, they prepare themselves to respond to any circumstance in a way that produces greater outcomes.

They don't make excuses; they find solutions to get better. Sports more than anything taught me the importance of accepting the many things that are beyond my control rather than dwelling on them. To continue to move forward effectively, we need to have not only that acceptance but also the ability to adjust our plan—whether that plan be a game plan for the night or a ten-year plan for our life. If we are too easily willing to surrender to a challenging situation every time that we can't move forward in the way we expected to, then we will continually be stopping short of our potential. Instead, finding what you can do among numerous uncontrollable challenges will not only help you continue to move forward but also help you grow more in the process.

Flexibility is more than just a physical necessity of athletes; it is a mental necessity too.

While I learned all these lessons from a game, I truly believe they have shown me more about how to live life away from the sport than anything else. As I move forward in the world, I take them with me to guide the way when things unexpectedly test me. While we make plans, the world plays by its own rules. There is no referee in life, policing things when they get unfair. You get tripped, hit, and knocked down, often without any warning. Throwing your hands up in the air and waiting for a penalty won't do you any good in the game of life. You can't go back and change the outcome. All you can do is accept it and move on. Move forward with purpose and intention. Don't simply react to the circumstances but respond to them with determination and do the next thing.

This philosophy has many benefits, as it focuses on embracing the discomfort that will undoubtedly exist in the uncontrollable world around us. Society today has an addiction to comfort, as Todd Kashdan and Robert Biswas-Diener point out in their book *The Upside of Your Dark Side*. We have become so developed that luxuries (think of things like air-conditioning, cars, and memory foam mattresses) have evolved into bare necessities and being physically comfortable is a primary desire that is fulfilled with relative ease. However, with that ability to satisfy our physical needs of comfort, we become less experienced at navigating challenges, which decreases our psychological resilience. As the authors suggest, there seems to be a direct relationship between physical comfort and our psychological comforts, or what are more commonly referred to as emotional states. "As we become more comfortable," the book explains, "researchers observed a related drop in our psychological health. Anxiety, in particular, seemed to be on the rise."

As we experience fewer hardships in our modern world, we become less equipped to handle challenges and manage the emotional and psychological impact of them when they do arise. From my perspective, sports help balance out that playing field. While we live a very comfortable and secure life, the obstacles that sports can cause keep us all mentally fit, enabling us to be stable and strong enough to withstand the turbulence. Overall, the willingness to accept and adapt to the discomfort of pain and hardships allows us to move through life with more resilience and optimism.

This lesson never became more valuable than during the coronavirus pandemic that hit the world with force in the spring of 2020. The months that followed resulted in the year 2020 itself becoming a cliché for bad news, lost opportunity, and obstacles beyond our control. The helplessness that everyone felt during this time created a tumultuous year with emotions hitting every low imaginable with momentum and force. In fact, many of the mental and emotional impacts of the pandemic were similar to the experiences of athletes who suffer from prolonged concussion symptoms, such as Crosby himself, that have been documented in research. Lack of clarity and control define the experiences for many. For athletes struggling with uncontrollable and lasting effects of their concussion, focusing not on the injury but instead on the recovery proved to be valuable for both their physical and mental well-being. In the pandemic, we have to do the same.

As I worked my way through the hardship of coaching in a pandemic, I realized that sometimes the most important thing you can do as a coach and leader isn't to say all the right things but to model the behavior and mindset you want your athletes to have. I spent that fall season actively searching for opportunities to not just tell my athletes what they could do to make the most of their season (or lack thereof) but show them. As the weeks rolled on, I implemented new and creative ways for the girls to improve in practice and to keep us engaged and excited. We did yoga, we played soccer tennis, and we competed weekly in formal scrimmages against ourselves. As November came, we were even preparing for our "senior game" to honor the seniors and livestream our scrimmage for their parents.

Our senior game week came, and along with it were a lot of concerned voices in the athletic department telling me I should reschedule because there was a snowstorm coming. I brought the concerns to our senior class and asked them what they preferred. We could move the game to earlier in the week (and not have our senior gifts and other fun surprises ready for them) or keep our game on Friday under the lights with a bit of snow. They all wanted Friday. They were all excited about an intense game under the lights in

November, and the weather just added to that effect. The weather and the lights were fun, but for me the key was that they were excited about something! That excitement was more valuable and rarer than ever before. I wasn't going to take that away too.

Thursday came, and we were told that the decision was no longer ours and our game had to be postponed. One more thing on the list. I had seniors on my team who were going remote after the weekend, and if we didn't play then, they would not get to be a part of their senior day. Saturday was the absolute latest we could have the game for them. It snowed Friday, and Saturday morning I received a text that there was too much snow left on the turf and we wouldn't be able to play. Cancel again on these girls? I couldn't do it.

"How many shovels do we have?" I texted back to our athletic director. I am sure the administration thought I had lost my mind, but in reality, I had just lost my patience. We couldn't control the weather, I get that. We couldn't control the pandemic, I knew. Things happen. But what was the next thing we could do? We might not be able to get rid of the virus in one day. We couldn't stop the snow from falling down out of the sky. But we could get rid of the snow after it fell. That we could do.

I looked out my window and saw the white blanket covering our turf field. For New England, it wasn't *that* much. It might not be easy or fun, but we could definitely take care of it. How could I constantly tell my team to focus on what they controlled, to dictate not what happened to them but how they responded to it, if I just accepted and lay down in defeat to a few inches of snow just sitting on the field?

Now, I didn't do it by myself—that would not have been possible in the time we had. But I also didn't tell anyone, besides my own team, to shovel the snow. I offered to do it myself. I sent out a few emails to gather up as many shovels as I could find on our small campus, and slowly but surely, as the morning hours passed along, more and more hands showed up on the turf to help. Administrators brought donuts and coffee. Even students who didn't play sports came down to move some snow. And while there were a few moments I thought for sure some people were cursing me under their breath with every pile of snow they moved for being the reason they were spending their Saturday morning shoveling a turf field, it was the happiest and proudest I had felt all fall.

"This is going to be impossible."

"There is so much left."

"The games are supposed to start in an hour."

"They couldn't have moved this snow yesterday?"

I heard a lot of comments being mumbled under people's breath that morning. Sure, maybe they could have moved it yesterday, but they hadn't. Yes, it felt impossible when we began, but every minute, more people came to help, making it feel more and more possible. Those people would not have come if we hadn't started. We suddenly regained some control of our situation. Yes, the games were a bit delayed, but you know what they weren't? Canceled. That afternoon, under the fifty-degree sun and surrounded by piles of snow, the football team and the boys' and girls' soccer teams were able to have a senior day.

Finding what you can do and how you can respond to a challenge isn't limited to rare circumstances like a pandemic. You can't change what has already happened, whether it be a virus, a snowstorm, an injury, a loss, or any other obstacle that might derail your plans and goals.

However, that next thing, your response, is all yours for the taking.

For me, what that 2020 season highlighted was that just because we have power over them doesn't mean the controllables are easy. They require real work. Sometimes it is the sweat and tears that are shed in the gym or on the field when you are pushing yourself to improve despite the lack of another opponent. Sometimes it is working out in your garage, or without equipment, because there is no other option. Sometimes it is simply showing up and giving it your all every day even when it feels like the world keeps handing you losses. Or it can be taking matters (or shovels) into your own hands to physically move pounds of snow so you can play. As it was falling from the sky on Friday, we couldn't stop it and we couldn't change the temperature outside. But once it was down, we had a choice. Managing difficult times and taking advantage of the things you can control is all about choosing well. When things happen and challenges arise, don't focus on whatever has already happened. Instead, choose to focus on the next thing you can do.

Lesson 6

THERE IS NO SUCH THING AS A SMALL IMPACT

As I have done more and more work with athletes, I have realized that many people have preconceived notions as to how we can impact a situation or an outcome. Some athletes have determined that if they don't score then they don't impact the game, or that if they don't play then they can't help the team. Those statements are entirely untrue. Everything we do and every situation we find ourselves in has an impact. If you choose to be purposeful and focus on positively impacting those around you with your actions, responses, and attitude, you can ultimately influence your surroundings more than your surroundings influence you.

This lesson became crucial when I was working with a hockey player who had a set identity as a goal scorer but wasn't scoring many goals or getting many opportunities on the ice in the offensive zone. When he first reached out to me early in the season, I had given him the assignment to text me three things he did well after every game, regardless of outcome or opportunity given to him. It was a challenge because he wasn't getting the chances that he felt like he deserved in regard to ice time—which created a pretty vicious cycle of thoughts and outcomes that were debilitating his confidence.

How am I supposed to perform well and make an impact on the game when I don't get the opportunity to do that? What can I really do well in a total of five quick shifts? I am a goal scorer, but the chances of me contributing on the score sheet when I am only on the ice during the penalty kill aren't too great. These are all questions and thoughts he didn't explicitly say to me, but he didn't have to. You could see all of that weighing down his face, shoulders, and overall demeanor. When an athlete begins to doubt themself, they spend most of their time looking at the ground rather than looking you in the eyes. Those thoughts don't need to be verbally spoken.

Therefore, when I first asked for a few things that he did well in his game, his initial response was "nothing." However, after a bit of prompting from me, he eventually was able to identify a few highlights, including his performance on the penalty kill and ability to break the puck cleanly out of the zone. "You may feel like if you're not scoring, you're not doing anything," I said to him. "But if that's the only asset in your game, you're not nearly as valuable as someone who is willing to also kill a penalty and break the puck out cleanly. It's not nothing. We have to start identifying the things you can do to impact the game when you get the chance, no matter how small that chance is. Because there's no such thing as a small impact."

The dictionary defines *impact* as "having a strong effect on someone or something; significant or major effect." *Small* is an antonym of *major*. Therefore, a small impact, by definition, is an oxymoron. You can make an impact in a variety of ways, none of which are more or less important than the others. If you took a championship team and removed one person from the team or organization, the one who made the "smallest" impact throughout the season, you could ultimately alter the course of the entire season and its outcome.

With each action, response, and decision we make, we are impacting ourselves and those around us. Now, it is important to acknowledge that an impact can be positive or negative, and that is the choice you get to make.

What type of impact do you want yours to be?

Take for instance Marc-André Fleury, the NHL goaltender who won three Stanley Cup championships alongside Sidney Crosby with the Pittsburgh Penguins. Fleury was the first overall draft pick in 2003. Only three goalies have been drafted first overall in the history of the NHL draft, and he was one of them. It was his ability in net that created a foundation that allowed the Penguins to build for success and win the Stanley cup in 2009. He was, without a doubt, the team's go-to goalie for years. But those other two championships in 2016 and 2017? Fleury watched his team win the Stanley Cup from the bench, while rookie Matt Murray stood in goal.

However, despite spending more time on the bench than the ice, you can't say that Fleury did not impact his team during those last two Stanley Cup victories. In fact, while many people wanted to try and create a storyline that pitted Fleury and Murray against each other like rivals, Murray himself is the first person to acknowledge the positive impact Fleury had on him and his performance during those two seasons. "He's been unbelievable," Murray said to reporters.[13] "I don't know where I would be without Fleury's mentorship, his advice." Fleury understood that the impact he could have as a friend and teammate to Murray was just as important as the impact he could have when given a chance on the ice. He knew that while his role was changing, his impact was not diminished.

For the athlete I was working with, in the games where he didn't get many opportunities on the ice, he would often reply to my text asking what he did well with things such as "staying positive and engaged on the bench" and "having a productive warm-up." Initially, I am sure he believed those things on his list were his not-so-subtle way of telling me he didn't impact the game. In his mind, how could he have? He didn't even get a fair chance in the actual game on the ice. However, what he slowly started to realize was that those aspects of his performance were just as important as the things he did on the ice during his shifts.

First and foremost, if he wasn't ready for the opportunities when they came, no matter how few and far between they may have felt, then *he* wasn't giving himself the best chance of embracing those opportunities.

You can't blame someone else for lack of opportunity if you are not ready for opportunities when they arise.

Once he made that realization, he was better able to approach his shifts with more confidence and readiness and impact the game in ways he had been wanting to all along, and in ways he knew he could. However, beyond the impact he was making on his own performance, his overall demeanor and attitude had the power to affect those around him, impacting his teammates and their overall performance whether he was playing or not. As a result, he was taking control and being a positive influence for his team rather than becoming a victim of the circumstances and letting the situation impact him.

The best teams, and the best coaches, know everyone makes an impact and values each member of the team, regardless of their status or visibility. The player who doesn't leave the bench is just as much a part of the team as the one in the starting lineup. The best athletes also know this and do their job to try to make a positive impact regardless of where they are in that lineup or the rank on any given day. Providing energy on the sidelines or increasing the compete level to make yourself and others better in practice isn't always the most glamorous role, but it is a role that is crucial to the success of any team.

As I was growing up, I saw the different ways people impacted the success of a team, or even the success of an individual. When I was younger, I didn't know how, but I always knew I wanted to be one of those people who made an impact. However, I knew I didn't have to be the one holding the trophy to be a part of the success. I wanted to be a part of the puzzle, even if it was just the tiniest piece, because from the experiences that I saw, there were no small pieces to the puzzle.

Every piece mattered in order to bring the vision to life.

Any puzzle with a missing piece will still be incomplete, regardless of how tiny that piece may be.

In 2018, the USA men's Olympic hockey team members wanted to acknowledge the numerous pieces of their puzzle and identify the various people who had an impact on their hockey careers that allowed them to fulfill a dream of making it onto the 2018 Olympic team. Every single member of that team, from the players and the coaches to the support staff, were tasked with calling someone from their past, whom they probably hadn't thanked before, who helped them get to the Olympics. The goal was to reach out to someone who would be surprised and excited to hear from them, not the people they talked to and thanked every day. While the purpose was to show gratitude to those whose impact may not always receive recognition, it also allowed them to reflect on and appreciate the journey that had led them to this great achievement.

That Olympic team was my dad's third Olympics, and he called Dave Peterson's wife, Janice. Dave was the head coach at the 1992 Olympics and had given my dad a big chance when he took him on his staff as his assistant that year, my dad's first Olympics. Dave had passed away, and other than a Christmas card every year, my dad hadn't talked to Janice in probably ten years, but he called to thank her in honor of Dave. He dialed her number from the airport terminal as the team was waiting to board the plane for PyeongChang. When Janice answered, she was floored by the unexpected call and deeply touched as the conversation brought her to tears. It had been twenty-six years since Dave had chosen my dad as his assistant and more than twenty years since he passed away, but he was still making an impact—not only through the opportunity he gave my dad but also the lessons my dad learned from that experience,which have been ever present throughout his coaching career and continuing Olympic experiences.

Other members of the team called youth coaches, former teammates, teachers, and many others who may not even have known that they played crucial roles in the success of these athletes and coaches. All people who had no chance of scoring a goal, getting a medal, or even winning a game at the Olympics, they were still significant players in the development, formation, and success of that team. Their impact was more than just important, it was life changing.

Lesson 7

GIVE EVERYTHING YOU GOT WHATEVER THAT MAY BE

While understanding your role and making an impact can require mental toughness, including resilience and focus, I have also seen extreme examples of physical toughness throughout my life. From grueling workouts to gritty displays in the game, I saw all the literal blood, sweat, and tears that went into athletic success. I vividly remember counting the stitches in my dad's head where he got hit by a puck, and watching numerous players, including my brother, attempting to pop their own shoulders back in place so they could go back in a game. After every game, countless bags of ice were handed out and strapped to body parts, and even the healthy players would walk with a limp and wince as they shrugged off concerns from family and friends. Hanging out at my friend's house, we watched as her dad put his food in a blender and then drank his dinner through a straw because his mouth was wired shut after blocking a shot with his face. He had a scissor or knife always in his pocket in case he got sick and had to cut open his mouth to throw up, so he wouldn't choke. The physical sacrifice of the game was always just a part of the process.

Due to that physical sacrifice, my job today has become a delicate balance of helping athletes protect their bodies and prioritize their health but also accept some of the physical challenges, pain and discomfort included, that will test them mentally and emotionally in their sport. Therefore, while the health world is attempting to shift the sports mentality away from the philosophy of "no pain, no gain," we can't deny that the pain will always be present to some degree. Muscle soreness is good and a sign you are getting stronger. If an athlete is only willing to play on the days that they feel 100 percent, then they will be left with very few days to play (some may even argue there will be no days left for them to play).

Humans frequently tend to view things from an all-or-nothing perspective. Our bodies feel great, or they are useless. Our energy is there, or it is not. Our performances are all good or all bad. Therefore, if people can't do everything, the next option for them is to do nothing. It is the same reason that people who are on diets and cheat at one meal typically end up cheating on the whole day or week. In reality, having one piece of cake wouldn't have a huge impact on your diet. If that one piece of cake leads to a whole day or week of other unhealthy food choices, suddenly that one piece of cake is detrimental to your goal.

Many elite-level athletes are perfectionists who embrace an all-or-nothing perspective when it comes to their performance. If they can't do their best, they don't want to do it. As a result, they may avoid situations that won't allow them to reach that impossible standard. On the flip side, however, this can also cause some to give their all and literally sacrifice their own mental and physical health to reach that ideal. Injuries become like a badge of honor. They are physical displays of how tough someone was or how much they were willing to give.

The reality is, whether you are healthy or not, the days

that you are going to feel 100 percent are rare. If you think you don't have all your energy or your best that day, so you give nothing, many days will be wasted. If you can instead focus on the 50, 60, or 70 percent that you are at and give every ounce of that, you are still making an impact.

Overall, mental performance is all about choices, and every day you get to decide how you use what you have.

That is what always amazed me the most at the end of a season. After the championship is won, the parades have happened, and the celebrations have settled, that's when the truth starts to leak out. The injuries that athletes were playing with, the adversity they had to battle through. They didn't tell you about it during the playoffs, not only because it would have been an advantage for the other team to know, but because it would have been a disadvantage for them to focus on it. Broken ribs, broken wrists, torn ligaments . . . being 100 percent isn't even a part of the discussion.

In 2004, Red Sox pitcher Curt Schilling's bloody sock became an iconic symbol of that physical sacrifice. With a torn tendon sheath, the Red Sox's medical team decided to do something they had never done before and temporarily bind Schilling's loose ankle tendon back into the skin so it was stable enough to allow him to pitch in game six of the American League Championship Series. Due to the procedure, his ankle started bleeding during the game, and his blood-soaked sock was visible to everyone. However, despite the injury, he helped the Red Sox complete their comeback, beating the Yankees after being down three games to none, the only team in MLB history to do so. They then went on to sweep the St. Louis Cardinals to become World Series champions.

Not every injury, however, is as visible as a blood-soaked sock. Tiger Woods won the US Open in 2008 with two stress fractures and a torn ACL in his left knee. Baseball player Kirk Gibson hit a two-run walk-off home run to help the Los Angeles Dodgers defeat the Oakland Athletics in the 1988 World Series with a pulled left hamstring and an injured right knee. In 1997, Michael Jordan played forty-four minutes and hit the game-winning three-pointer for the Chicago Bulls against the Utah Jazz, all while suffering from food poisoning. Athletes constantly push their bodies to their absolute limits.

As I embarked on my own athletic career, I was fortunate enough to not suffer any major injuries, but my siblings both battled their own bodies throughout their experiences. Shoulders, knees, collarbones, faces—they all have been pushed, sewed, or screwed back together. It gives them both a little bit more street cred than I have when it comes to our athletic identities. I never knew the struggle. I didn't sacrifice as much for the glory. For that I am grateful, but also weirdly a little jealous. It is like when my sister fell off a horse for the first time when she was younger and one of the older riders came up to her and said, "Welcome to the club. You're officially a real rider." Then, instead of crying, my sister stood up with pride and got back on the horse.

It is difficult to understand why the physical sacrifice feels like a fundamental part of that identity, but it does. The same way hazing rituals have been able to trigger this sense of belonging rooted deep within our brains, suffering makes us value something more than if it was easily acquired. The cognitive dissonance you would experience if you went through all that trouble for something you didn't care about

Earn it.

would be too great. Therefore, your brain shifts and convinces you that it is in fact all worth it. If you have to earn it, that makes it special. When you have something that you are willing to suffer for and you know that the person next to you is willing to do the same, that is both motivating and unifying.

In fact, research has demonstrated this unifying element of pain in a series of studies that identified pain as "social glue."[14] Experiments in the research had groups doing a variety of mundane tasks with varying degrees of pain, induced by things such as extreme cold water and physical challenges. The results showed that participants in the groups who had an element of pain felt more connected to their group and were more willing to cooperate to benefit the group rather than only themselves. This demonstrates how the pain and suffering in sports, whether it be an injury or simply a grueling workout, can be fundamental to the team element of sports, making us feel both connected and committed.

More specifically, the pain makes the result that much sweeter both for the group and for the individual. Our experiences are all relative, and after having gone through the worst, the best becomes infinitely greater by comparison. For instance, I hate running, but my favorite part of the run is the end when I am done and have completed my goal. That mixture of exhaustion, elation, and accomplishment wouldn't exist or feel nearly as good if I didn't have the painful moments in the process to compare it to. For many athletes, that first game or that first goal back after an injury that tested both their physical and mental toughness is an indescribable joy. Frequently referred to as a rush that you wouldn't be able to find anywhere else, the trials and

Pain + suffering can be fundamental to the team element of sport.

tribulations athletes face are worth it for the highs they are striving to reach, that elusive reward at the end.

Famous psychologist B. F. Skinner used to study the effect of rewards on behavior using his famous Skinner box. It was a small chamber where animals would be rewarded with food for simply pressing a lever. Throughout his research, Skinner would manipulate how frequently the animals would be rewarded. In some trials, they would receive food every time they pressed the lever or after a fixed number of times, for instance every fifth or tenth time they pressed the lever. In other trials, the rewards came at random, leaving the animal without any certainty of when they would receive the food. While some people assume the consistent reward would result in more consistent behavior, the findings actually showed the opposite. If animals don't know when the next reward will come, then they display higher rates of response. In other words, they press the lever more frequently when they don't know if they will be rewarded or not. This is similar to the reward schedule used in slot machines.

In a way, sports have become a constructive outlet for this innate human desire to gamble for the possibility of a reward. While the world around us has evolved greatly, our brains, which were hardwired to motivate us to find food for survival, are still ever present on the athletic field. You could apply the same concept of the Skinner box and explain the persistent and oftentimes irrational determination displayed by athletes to achieve a goal. The simple possibility or hope of scoring the goal or making the team or winning the medal is more motivating to the behavior than a guaranteed reward. Especially if an athlete has experienced some success, and the high that comes along with that, they will spend an extensive amount of time continuing to try to chase that dream to experience it again. The reward causes an almost addiction-like cycle that pushes them through any physical pain. They don't know when, or if ever, they will experience it again, but the chance that it might only take one more try, one more shot, one more season, makes it hard to walk away.

As a result of this persistence, I have worked with athletes who have pushed their bodies to the edge. They have broken their backs, suffered concussions, and lost their literal senses (both feeling and hearing) throughout their bodies. Part of our process together is focused on managing the unexpected detours, delays, and roadblocks that appear because of those injuries. As we have learned, things happen and we need to accept that they happen before we can shift our focus on moving forward and doing the next thing. However, once we do that, we work on becoming more self-aware so we can read and understand the signals our bodies are sending us. That way, we can intelligently push ourselves but also protect ourselves and be smart in the process.

Sometimes, however, the battle isn't always physical.

You can experience pain and fatigue that are both emotional and mental. While those challenges are just as real as the physical ones, you can push through those too. I remember one day before training I had an athlete approach me to let me know she had had a bad day and didn't think she had enough energy, physically or mentally, to practice that day. As I made it clear that it was her choice and I would support her decision, I also tried to explain to her that even if she only had 50 percent of her usual ability, it would be 50 percent more training than she would get if she sat out. Just the act of moving her body and increasing her heart rate would be good for her as an athlete, and more importantly, it would most likely increase her overall energy level and mood. If she chose to play, I would accept whatever she had to give that day, as long as she gave me all of it. After some thought, she decided to show up. While it was clear on the field that it wasn't her best day, she gave us what she had and got a little bit stronger that day, both physically and mentally.

Desiree Linden, who in 2018 became the first American woman to win the Boston marathon in three decades, knows how rare a great day is when it comes to training and competing. The day she crossed the finish line first on Boylston Street was described by most as cold, wet, and windy. Linden herself even said that it was "pretty miserable out" when asked about the harsh weather conditions and that she didn't feel her best at times in the race and contemplated dropping out.[15] However, despite all the reasons not to, she showed up. Almost a year later, in a video created alongside Brooks Running, Linden narrates as she is seen going for a run.[16] "Running isn't about good days and bad days," she explains. "Running is cumulative. Runs are collected every time you tie up your laces. And there's only one rule for success: keep showing up." This is not just true for running.

Giving it your all doesn't guarantee a result. It doesn't guarantee a goal, a medal, or even a spot on the team. But the more you focus on what you give, and what you put into the process, the less important the actual outcome becomes. In whatever you are working toward, your days add up.

The little moments, the tiniest efforts, and even the smallest steps help progress you toward your goal.

It doesn't have to be your best day to make you better.

Lesson 8

YOUR PRIDE COMES FROM YOUR PROCESS

In 1998, when I was six years old, the USA women's hockey team made history at the Winter Olympics in Nagano, Japan, by beating Canada to win the first ever women's hockey team gold medal. Leading up to those Olympics, the USA team was training in Massachusetts. A few times a month during that time, my dad would drive up to their training facility from Cape Cod, where we were then living year-round, to work with the goalies. As a result, when they won, I asked my dad if they could come celebrate with us. Turns out, someone could.

A few weeks after returning home from Nagano, local gold medalist A. J. Mleczko took the short flight from Nantucket Island to the Hyannis airport on Cape Cod, where my best friend and I greeted her on the tarmac. Although my personal connection to A. J. was limited, she greeted us like we were her own friends. I beamed with pride as we escorted what I was sure would be the greatest show-and-tell item in history to my school, where she spoke not just to my class but to the entire school. She talked about her Olympic experience and winning the gold medal and showed off that shiny new accessory hanging from her neck. I remember as she graciously took it off her own neck and let everyone who wanted to touch it, hold it, and wear it. It was passed around like any old show-and-tell item would be.

Many of the parents and teachers in attendance seemed very nervous and asked her if she truly felt comfortable allowing clumsy elementary school kids to pass around her gold medal like a hot potato. She laughed and responded by telling us all a story. As one may assume, after you win a gold medal, there are a lot of events for you to go to and show off your hard-earned piece of jewelry. At these events, people frequently ask to see the medal and hold it and even wear it. A. J. had allowed some nice person to hold her medal, and that person, who I am sure felt horrible about it, dropped it.

Turns out, gold isn't as tough as the athletes that compete for it.

The tumble to the ground left the gold medal dented and damaged—just a few days old and already scarred. Six-year-old me was horrified when I heard the story. I thought about my sister, who didn't even like to scuff or dirty her sneakers when she was wearing them. Now dented, that precious gold medal was destroyed. It was no longer any good. Imagine working so hard for something and having it get blemished so soon after earning it, especially in such an unnecessary way. No wonder she was letting a bunch of kids wear her medal; at this point, who cares anymore.

She laughed as she told the story, and the adults around me eventually did too. I was confused by their reactions. Then she continued to talk about her team, their experience, and how proud they were. While I never forgot that story, I more importantly never forgot her response to it. Her lack of concern for the medal itself was because her pride wasn't tied to that pretty, shiny medallion, but to her journey. Yes, she was proud of what she accomplished, but she seemed prouder of everything they did as a team along the way.

Pride is discussed frequently when you work with athletes or performers. Ultimately, it is a topic anyone at any age in any context can relate to. Making parents proud, making friends, teachers, coaches, or bosses proud—it is a universal human desire. Pride, even at six years old, I understood. What I was just beginning to understand, however, was that you could be proud of so much more than an outcome or a result. It was a lesson I had been introduced to that day and many times before, but it was one that I would have to relearn numerous times throughout my life.

Ask a gold medalist where their medal is, and a majority of them will have some insignificant answers: an underwear drawer, a closet, some may not even be sure. Ask an Olympic medalist about their experience, and you will receive a long and detailed response that most likely doesn't mention the medal at the end. More importantly, ask any Olympian what they are proud of, and while that medal may be mentioned, because to them it represents so much more than a placement on a podium, I highly doubt it will be their primary focus.

Take swimmer Caeleb Dressel, a seven-time Olympic gold medalist, for example. During his time in Tokyo at the 2020 Summer Olympics (which were held during the summer of 2021 due to the coronavirus pandemic), Caeleb was interviewed for the *Today Show*. In the segment, interviewer Craig Melville asked Caeleb, "What would you consider success in Tokyo?" Without hesitation, Caeleb responded, "If I learned something from the meet, to move forward into next year, if I learn something about myself as a man, as a person, as an athlete, as a swimmer, I'll be happy with it." Clearly surprised, Melville questioned why Caeleb didn't even mention the podium or a medal in his response. Confidently, Caeleb responded, "It's not about that for me. I don't keep any of that stuff. You guys should be jealous. I get to do the fun part, which is racing. . . . I don't need a piece of metal to remind me of that. I got to enjoy it."

It isn't a medal or a trophy—the "it" that he is referring to is the race, the process, and the whole experience. If you take the time to listen to other successful athletes discuss their careers, you will begin to notice that when people are proud of something, they enjoy talking about it. What you also notice is that these champions spend less time talking about the actual medal moment than any other part of their journey.

While we often try to make others proud, the most challenging recipient of pride can sometimes be ourselves. How do we make ourselves proud? How do we succeed and become an inspiration and make it all worth it? If it doesn't come from the gold medal, resting in the bottom of a junk drawer somewhere in your house all battered and bruised, where do we find it, or how do we create it? What do we truly become proud of?

That is where many athletes and coaches, including myself, who are striving to achieve and accomplish great things, need to shift their perspective away from that final outcome. As it turns out, your pride doesn't reside in your results, but stems from the grueling and oftentimes punishing, but oh so rewarding process: the days you were too tired to train but did it anyway; the mistakes you made along the way that didn't stop you from continuing on.

"Picture yourself standing on the podium," I often tell the athletes I am working with today. Imagine the weight of that gold medal hanging around your neck, everyone cheering for you, proud of your accomplishment. Now imagine all the feelings and thoughts you would have in that moment. Most likely you imagine a sense of pride, mixed with exhaustion, excitement, elation . . . and I would bet you imagine those feelings with a sense of accomplishment, replaying the hours of preparation, practice, and hard work that got you to that moment. Now hold that thought, and imagine the same moment, but take away the journey. Remove every challenge, battle, mistake, or obstacle you had to overcome. Take away all the tears, all the pain, and all the laughter. Imagine, you walked into the Olympics without trials and were handed the medal. How proud do you feel now?

Lesson 9

WHERE YOU ARE DOESN'T CHANGE WHAT YOU DO

As I was growing up, soccer was undeniably one of the biggest parts of my life. While it was a constant I could rely on, it also brought me into many unfamiliar situations. New teams, new schools, new groups of friends, and new experiences were all introduced to me because of the game I played. However, whenever I was outside of my comfort zone, I could always ground myself in the familiarity of the game that made me feel at home. In a new place, filled with new and unrecognizable faces, it was the one thing I felt comfortable with. It gave me an automatic sense of belonging in places I didn't actually belong just yet.

During my freshman year of high school, for instance, I remember feeling so young and insecure compared to the seniors on my team all season. In school and at team gatherings, thirteen-year-old me frequently felt out of place with some girls who were already eighteen. On the field, however, I felt transformed. I was confident and in charge. I belonged and I didn't doubt it. Soccer always seemed to give me that sense of security I didn't find in many places as a self-conscious teenager. Then after that year, my family moved, and I would find myself at two new schools and on multiple new teams before I graduated high school.

In life, especially as a teenager, you are constantly trying to find where you fit in. Growing up can seem like a constant search for your place in the world, or even just your place at the lunch table in the cafeteria. We constantly place labels on items that we want to claim as our own as we construct our identities around them. That's my seat, or that's my classroom—objects that provide the same comfort as our home, giving us a place to belong. That was soccer for me. It was my sport, my thing, my place.

While the context around me constantly shifted during my adolescence, I always found my bearings on a grass field between two goals. No matter how out of my element I felt, I knew what do with a ball at my feet. I didn't have to change that or reinvent the game just because my jersey was a different color or the field was in a city that was new to me. I just had to do the same things I had been doing for most of my life—play soccer. That realization not only helped me adjust to the frequent changes I experienced in high school but also helped me find a lot of success on the soccer field and molded me into a consistent and reliable player.

Maybe that is why I felt so much guilt for walking away when I did. It was as if I was abandoning my own home, the place that made me who I was.

However, roots don't exist to keep you close to the ground and stuck in one place. Their purpose is to nourish you and allow you to grow in multiple different directions.

Like a hermit crab that leaves its shell to find a bigger home, we all eventually outgrow our place that kept us safe for so long and have to leave that comfort zone in order to find a new place with more room for us to reach new heights. However, unlike that shell that a hermit crab leaves behind, those roots are always there, not only reminding us of our foundation and keeping us sturdy in the wind, but welcoming us back if we ever have the desire to return.

Those roots can also help high performers steady their minds when they find themselves on a stage bigger than they've ever experienced before. Rasmus Dahlin, for instance, was the first overall pick in the 2018 NHL draft. The highly anticipated prospect had all eyes on him as he was considered the savior the Buffalo Sabres needed to rebuild their franchise. However, at media events such as the NHL combine, where people questioned him about the expectations and pressure that would exist once he was officially drafted, Dahlin was quoted more than once as saying, "It's just hockey."[17] While everything else in his life was about to change, including moving to a new country, Dahlin found comfort and excitement in the game he had been playing his whole life.

Cori "Coco" Gauff, American tennis player, employed similar tactics on the big stage at Wimbledon in 2019. After beating her idol Serena Williams in the opening round, then fifteen-year-old Gauff acknowledged the magnitude of the venue and the event but found comfort in the familiarity that existed even in a situation that felt so new. "I've never played on a court so big," Gauff said.[18] "I had to remind myself that the lines on the court are the same size. Everything around it might be bigger, but the lines are the same." Being the youngest player ranked in the World Tennis Association's top one hundred players in the world, reaching a career-high ranking of seventeenth in January 2022, Gauff has had her career take her places that could easily overwhelm even the mentally toughest athletes. However, she realized the importance of sticking to what she knew.

The more both athletes and coaches accomplish in their

sport, the more places and unfamiliar situations they find themselves in on and off the field, and those new things can cause a lot of internalized pressure. Negative thoughts, expectations, and uncertainties flood the brain when you are outside of your comfort zone. A new city, a new team, a new experience can throw you into uncharted territory that fills you with fears and anxiety. As a result, many athletes struggle in strange environments because they let so much of their context throw them off their game. Newfound media attention, flashing lights, bigger crowds—all these things can cause an athlete to overthink their performance and to question their every move, a process that not only slows down their reaction time but impairs the accuracy of their decision-making. The reality is that none of those external things changed anything about the game itself.

Even coaches can get caught up in the pressures of a new environment. I have heard of so many coaches who change up their whole game plan when the playoffs start or when they make it to a big tournament. Practices and plays suddenly look different as they try to prepare their players for the big game. Not only do these alterations throw off their athletes, but they send a message that this is different than what they've been doing at a time when they want their athletes to be consistent and confident. No one is confident doing something they've never done before.

Rather than focusing on what is new, rely on the things that are old and familiar, the things you know—the game itself.

Give your team confidence by helping them see themselves in that winning performance because they've been doing it all along, just playing the game they know how to play. You may be somewhere you've never been before, but you're doing something you know how to do.

A lot of that familiarity and comfort can be found in those routines that you have created both as teams and as individuals. Your pregame process should not shift because the stakes are higher. As you go through motions that you have done countless times, you should feel yourself find a sense of ease even in the most pressure-filled environments. It will not only bring you back to a place of confidence and comfort but also shift your focus back to the task at hand and not the external distractions.

That's how it went for me. As my life continued to shift and change, my identity connected to soccer gave me stability that circumstances couldn't provide. My junior year in high school, as my parents drove away and I watched from my dorm room window after they dropped me off at boarding school for the first time, tears hovered along the edges of my eyes. I didn't have time to cry, though, because I had practice that was about to start. So, I took a deep breath, grabbed my bag, and ran out to the field. On new teams, in new places, with new people, the intimidation, discomfort, and fear I felt would usually disappear once the ball started rolling. At every school I attended, I would get lost in the hallways or around the campus, but the lines on that field always looked the same. I knew my way around there. I was able to find home even in the most uncharted territories.

Lesson 10

TO DO IT WELL
FIRST YOU HAVE TO HAVE
THE COURAGE TO DO IT AT ALL

While soccer provided me with a safe place in my life, I lived carefully within the boundaries of that comfort zone. I became extremely talented at identifying my limits and sticking to them rather than pushing myself past them. I tried out for teams I was fairly confident I would make. I applied to boarding schools I was confident I could get into. In fact, in my memory I have never received a rejection letter from a school or not made a team. While back then that was a source of pride, today I'm not as proud of that accomplishment. I sometimes wonder where I could have ended up if I had aimed a little higher and risked my self-confidence a bit more.

I liked to be good at things and do them well, and I still do. While I enjoyed the process of soccer and valued everything from the journey it provided me, I really enjoyed the traditional definition of success. Not having experienced too much struggle or failure up until that point in my life, when I first received the infamous summer workout packet leading up to college preseason, I was intimidated but not threatened. I was never the fastest on any of my teams, but I was also fit from always playing on multiple teams. I had also spent years watching my sister follow her summer workout program for her Division I soccer team, even working out with her sometimes. Except then I always had the luxury of picking and choosing when to go, and it never mattered if I actually achieved the goals set by the coach. This time, it mattered. This time, those benchmarks were setting the expectations for me.

My summer started off with motivation and determination. I began my summer workout program before my summer even started. Still at boarding school, one morning my friend and I woke up at 6:00 a.m. before class and went to the turf. However, while I was in shape, what I quickly realized was that I was nowhere near the shape I had to be in. Suddenly, fear of possible failure set in. My focus shifted away from the process and straight to the outcome. What if I'm not actually good enough? What if I never meet these benchmarks? Rather than pushing my boundaries, I decided to retreat. I knew about all the hard work and failure that go into athletic success, but just because we know some things to be true doesn't mean we always apply them effectively to our own lives. While I had seen others push themselves to be their best my whole life, I had never truly had to push myself before. Turned out, I wasn't very good at it.

Fast-forward two months, and I was standing on the turf with twenty other girls I'd just met. Before we even got to touch a ball, we had to do the beep test. The beep test is a fitness test consisting of running back and forth and making sure you reach the end before the beep on a recording. As time progresses, the beeps get closer and closer together. Standing on the line waiting for the recording to start, I felt panic inside me, like the kid sitting in school watching the teacher hand out a test she didn't study for. Except this wasn't a multiple-choice test where I still had a 25 percent chance of getting a correct answer each time.

Suddenly I felt my legs shake. I always thought that was a figure of speech, but I remember being genuinely concerned my legs weren't going to work. I have never been the unprepared kid. This was a foreign situation for me. When I was done, I wasn't even out of breath. I just couldn't make my legs move any faster. I had worked out all summer, yes. But I basically read the SparkNotes instead of the whole book to prepare for the test. Rather than motivating me to work harder, the anxiety I felt all summer about this moment caused me to avoid the issue. Subconsciously, I figured if I didn't try my hardest then I couldn't feel bad if I didn't pass.

Of course, I failed the fitness test. I knew I would. But imagine how I would have felt if I had worked my hardest all summer and then failed the test. Years later, as a teacher, I would have a conversation with an advisee of mine who said she didn't want to study because she knew she was going to fail her test anyway. The test was unfair, and the teacher was too hard. She had every reason she would fail clearly outlined. If she spent all this time studying and preparing and still failed, she would feel way worse about herself than if she just failed without trying. As I stood in her doorway listening to her logic, I felt how I imagine parents feel when their kids reflect the most frustrating attributes of themselves. I just shook my head at her and told her I got it, but that failing was guaranteed without the studying, and if she studied at least she'd have a chance. She enthusiastically disagreed, and I left her alone because some lessons we have to learn ourselves.

Part of those lessons and growing pains is imperfection. You won't do things well the first time, and maybe not even the second or third.

I can guarantee you won't make any mistakes if you never try, but I can also guarantee that you will never succeed or do it well either.

For athletes who strive for perfection, this can be one of the most painful parts of the growth process. For a figure skater, for instance, who is judged and scored on their performance, losing points for every imperfection, it takes up even more space in their mind than an athlete who can mess up but fight back to even the score.

One winter, I was working with a figure skater who was incorporating more challenging jumps into her program. While she was struggling to complete these new jumps, she wanted to make it her goal to attempt them each day. I quickly stopped her. "What is the difference between attempting something and just doing it?" I asked her.

"Well, I haven't done it successfully yet," she explained, "so I think this will take off the pressure of feeling like I need to do it successfully right away." I liked her thought process but was worried about how that mindset could impact her progress.

"What is one of the biggest mistakes you make when you go into a jump that causes you to fall or be unsuccessful at it?" I responded.

"I don't jump through it. I hesitate a bit," she said. I thought for a second. "Wouldn't setting a goal that requires you to jump through it be more effective than one that allows you to not commit to the jump?"

I liked her rationale for her goal, but I didn't think it was the best decision. I agreed that we didn't want her goals to focus on landing the jump either. We didn't need to add pressure to the final product. However, by claiming she just wanted to attempt something, she left too much room to talk herself out of doing it. Trying and doing your best are two different things that people like to pretend are the same. You can try and only give it 50 percent. I wanted her to go on the ice and do her best. I didn't care if she landed it. I didn't care if she did the jump well or if the result was an ugly mess that would have a million deductions at competition. She needed to just jump. If she attacked the jump in the air, she would find more results than if she just tried—not only because it is more dangerous to hesitate when you go into the jump, but because she would be creating her own confidence and determination.

"Even with the word *attempt*, you are hyper-focused on the outcome," I emphasized to her as our conversation continued. "I want you to worry less about what the jump looks like and just go for it.

Overall, we need to care less and do more.

Care less about the results, or what other people think, or what the judges might say, and just go after it." Former number-one golfer in the world Rory McIlroy has echoed this mindset when asked about the approach to his golf game. "I'd rather fail by trying 100% than by sort of holding back and maybe not giving myself the opportunity to do well," McIlroy has been quoted saying.[19] "So I'm committed to making sure, even if I don't play my best golf and shoot the scores I want, I'm going to go down swinging and I'm going to go down giving it my best."

Just like I had spent that summer preparing for preseason, I tried to do the fitness tests on my own, but I didn't give it my best each day I was out on that field. I was worried my best wouldn't result in the desired outcome, so I casually attempted it with little emphasis on making the set times. I wasn't brave enough to just jump right in, give it my all, and be OK with being bad at it. Once the figure skater started to care less about the outcome, she began improving on her jumps and qualified for nationals as a senior skater for the first time.

The words we use are powerful, and how we phrase things can influence our perceptions of reality and our mindset. Studies have demonstrated how critical phrasing is in goal setting specifically, setting clear guidelines for how we should approach this crucial process. For instance, always put your goals in the affirmative; focus on what you want to accomplish, not what you want to avoid. For my athlete, it was not to attempt a goal but to do a goal. We can assess how well you did it after and adjust if necessary. However, it is not just in goal-setting that our words are important. When I connect with my athletes and check in on their progress, I don't ask for positives and negatives from their week. Instead, I ask them to give me their highlights and a challenge. While the challenge may be the same as their "negative," a challenge is something that we overcome. Not only does it prime them to view it as that, but it also helps them automatically discuss how they managed it or overcame it, without me prompting them to.

Words are also critically important for coaches to consider when they are communicating with their team or individual athletes. You can communicate the same thing in many different ways, and everything from the words you choose to the tone you take can impact the response you get from your athletes.

Lesson 11

THERE IS A DIFFERENCE BETWEEN LISTENING AND HEARING

When it comes to communication, hearing and listening are not the same thing. Hearing is the sensation of sound. Listening is what happens when you decide to pay attention to and process things in a way that allows them to influence your actions and thoughts. It is one of the most important skills both athletes and coaches can have. First off, it will help you communicate more effectively within a team, but it can also allow you to intentionally navigate through some of the criticism and opinions you will inevitably face.

I was on many teams, and I would call my athletic experience a very cultured one. I have had quite a worldly soccer education, with coaches from England, Scotland, Ireland, New Zealand, and Brazil, to name a few. These international coaches always had incredible soccer IQs, coming from countries where soccer was the primary sport. Their understanding of the game was unparalleled, and it was quite obvious they spent their whole lives both watching and playing the game. These guys always had a bit of an edge, but their passion was contagious, and they were some of the most fun coaches I ever played for.

However, every experience I had with my coaches was not

always filled with fun and positivity. One of the most common and unfavorable traits of my coaches was their screaming. You could hear them from anywhere on the field. As a matter of fact, you could probably hear them from three fields away. Yelling expletives with their hands up in the air, some pacing barefoot up and down the muddy sideline, is how I will always remember these coaches. Despite how much their aggressive style annoyed me, it never bothered me so much that it hindered my performance on the field like it did some of my teammates. In fact, no matter how loud they were on the sidelines, on the field I could barely even hear them. Growing up, my parents used to tell me I had selective hearing. I don't think at the time they meant it as an advantage, but on those teams it was. However, it wasn't so much selective hearing as it was selective listening.

This skill of tuning out, or not listening to, the unnecessary auditory information seems to surprisingly be just another element of athleticism. Though not a physical trait, it is an act that athletes have shown to have more ability to do than non-athletes. In fact, in a study done at Northwestern University in 2019, Division I athletes were found to be better able to respond to auditory signals than their non-athlete counterparts.[20] Their ability was visible not just in their responses but also in their brain activity. However, rather than tuning in or turning up the signals from the target sound, like musicians have been found to do, the brain activity of the athletes revealed that they turned down the nonessential auditory signals, thus minimizing the brain's background noise. This allowed them to better pinpoint the sound they wanted to hear.

This process in the brain was all done subconsciously, without the athletes being aware that they were doing it. In other words, if the athlete knows what they want to focus on, their brain automatically silences the rest and doesn't listen to it. On the field, this could explain why an athlete can listen to their coach or their teammate giving them instructions from across the field even in a loud and crowded stadium or why a basketball player can hear the ball bounce and make a free throw shot among taunting and jeers from the opposing team's fans.

As an athlete, you can't shut off your senses, and you will still be able to hear everything around you. However, listening to the right things is of the utmost importance. The constructive feedback and guidance that is provided to you, the support and advice from those around you, and input from teammates and your coaches are all crucial in your ability to work together and move toward your goals. You have to pay attention to what others are saying so you can process it effectively and respond with the appropriate words or actions. As a coach, you are expected to do the same. You need to be able to listen to the many voices that exist within your team so you can offer the best possible solutions and support.

However, listening to everything you can hear as an athlete is not going to benefit you. Not only is that too much information for you to process while trying to perform, not all that information will be advantageous for you to internalize. Although coaches will try to tell you the things that they think you need in the moment, they don't always get it right. Like my passionate coaches screaming at me from the other side of the field, I subconsciously could hear enough to know when I needed to listen but didn't process their words unless it was instructional. Even teammates can express frustration that can be detrimental to your mindset at times. You want to make sure to tune in to the helpful feedback or encouragement and tune out any negative emotional reactions that might derail your focus.

Mentally categorizing the things that won't help as non-essential auditory information, like in the Northwestern study, will allow your brain to mute them along with the rest of the background noise. Although the process in your brain is subconscious, you can take steps to induce that response in your brain by staying disciplined in your focus. The things that you choose to actively pay attention to and prioritize will become the things your brain listens to. Allocate your time and attention to the helpful feedback. One of the easiest ways to do this is by directing your eyes to the sources of that valuable information. That basketball player taking the free throw isn't looking at the crowd behind the hoop that is cheering and chanting. Instead, their eyes are focused on the ball and the noise it makes as it bounces off the floor back into their hands.

You can hear the rest in the background, but you don't have to listen.

In addition to the noise in the moment of a competition, there are constant distractions that exist off the field or away from the arena. Spectators, opponents, and commentators will often say things they think you don't want to hear to try to evoke a reaction, and media outlets and social media have made it easier for those thoughts and comments to reach the athlete at any given time. The noise can be hard to avoid. You will be around it and will inevitably hear it, but don't give it the attention that allows your brain to listen to it. Instead, listen to the things you want to hear. As you are preparing for a game, that might be a pregame playlist, your own voice, or the support from those around you.

In order to help them maintain their focus, many athletes today actually take steps to actively eliminate some of the noise in their environment when they are performing before it can even get into their brain, a trend we saw emerge at the 2020 Olympic Games in Tokyo. Australian swimmer Ariarne Titmus, who won two gold medals, a silver, and a bronze in Tokyo, deleted every social media app on her phone during the competition. "I think as much as messages from everyone [are] really beautiful and it's good to look at a little bit," Titmus said, "it can sometimes be a bit overwhelming."[21] Swimmer Caeleb Dressel, mentioned before, also said he was off Instagram during those Olympics.

In addition to Titmus and Dressel, USA gymnast Suni Lee openly discussed the direct impact she believes social media had on her performance.[22] After winning gold in the all-around competition, she admitted to getting a bit distracted by her sudden social media fame, which led to a lack of focus and some uncharacteristic mistakes, resulting in her settling for a bronze in the uneven bars final, her strongest event. In just the short week and a half since the start of the Olympics, Lee had gained almost one million new followers on her Instagram account. That following came with a lot more comments, voices, and overall noise.

Whether you are an athlete or a coach, or neither, you will experience times when people criticize you. In addition, you will experience times when people praise you. You'll hear it all from where you are, but none of it really benefits you. The attention, the comments, and the opinions are all noise. You need to identify what information coming in will help you move forward and listen closely to that. Then allow your brain to turn down the rest of the static.

Lesson 12

YOUR GREATEST RESOURCE WILL ALWAYS BE YOURSELF

With all the noise that will surround you in life, the most powerful influence will always be yourself. Sure, there will be a lot of other people who can impact you if you let them, in both good and bad ways, but none so much so as the person staring back at you in the mirror. For me, when I walked away from soccer in college, there were a lot of places I wanted to point my finger to place the blame of my perceived downfall as far away from myself as possible. I was frustrated, disappointed, and most importantly not responsible. However, as tempting as it was for me to focus solely on my coach or the environment I was in, I couldn't do that.

Even with the power that my coach's position gave him, I still had more power over my actions and responses. At first, I did what I thought was expected of me: I put my head down, I kept quiet, and I worked. My mentality was more serious than probably ever before in a soccer environment, and while I thought my composed and stoic demeanor around soccer might impress and gain respect from my coach, it did little to that effect. However, while I had the right intentions, I was also too stubborn to adjust when my approach didn't work. Instead of reaching out, asking for help or feedback, I doubled down and kept my coach at a distance. Although he didn't make me feel supported or welcome, I also didn't reach out for the support that may have existed, worsening the problem for no one else but myself. I wanted so badly to prove to him that I deserved to be there that I attempted to do it on my own. I wanted to show him that I didn't need his help.

There are always plenty of problems for those of us who are looking for them. Whether it is something impeding your plan for the day or your plan for your life, obstacles will present themselves. I had plenty of challenges that fall my freshman year of college, but what I wasn't aware of or willing to see was the important role that I played.

The solution to my struggle, the resource I wasn't tapping into, was myself.

Unfortunately, too often when we get lost in the darkness of frustration, disappointment, or fear, we lament over the misfortune of the night and don't realize we have a flashlight in our hand. While the flashlight won't illuminate the whole room, it can help guide us through without bumping into so many obstacles.

As an athlete and a person, I was always so intrigued by others that I didn't reflect on myself as often as I know we all should. Fascinated and inspired by the successful athletes and coaches I grew up around, I was more curious about what motivated them and others than about what was motivating me. I was fascinated by the variety that existed in people's responses and reactions to their environment. While I analyzed my own teammates, my coaches, and my surroundings, I didn't spend enough time on myself.

Possibly this was because reflecting on everyone else was less intimidating than dissecting my own thoughts and behaviors, but I also think it was partly because I took myself for granted. Thinking about myself was less interesting because I assumed that I already knew everything about myself. What I know now is that knowing yourself requires just as much, if not more, time and work than understanding others. As a result of overlooking my own inner workings as an athlete, when things became challenging for me it was difficult for me to articulate how I was feeling and why: the avoidant behavior I exhibited that summer out of fear and the silence that followed that season as frustration boiled beneath the surface. More importantly, I didn't know how to effectively manage them in a way that would motivate me through them.

The more I work with other athletes, the more I indirectly end up working on myself and reflecting personally on my own strengths and weaknesses and the challenges that I face. This process has allowed me to better manage my difficult days and find motivation when I need it, but it has also allowed me to be more patient and forgiving with myself when things aren't going the way I want and frustration starts to build. Most importantly, through this work is how I have learned that failure has always been one of my biggest fears that frequently held me back. Since acknowledging that to myself, I have been able to purposefully put myself in more situations that push me outside of my comfort zone and allow me (or force me) to experience failure. The more I make mistakes, the more accepting I become of myself, but also the more things I am able to achieve and learn.

 Knowing yourself is one of the most underrated and undervalued types of knowledge that a human can have. When working with athletes, I spend a lot of time focusing on self-awareness and personal reflection. We reflect not only on the things we believe define us as a person and a player, such as our strengths and weaknesses, but also on the emotions we feel, the thoughts we have, and the moments that we find most challenging. If we don't know those things about ourselves, trying to find solutions will be like trying to find your way out of a maze that doesn't have an outlet. There is no clear path or destination.

Part Two

EMOTIONS

" *Emotions are like that cold water: they can be intimidating at first. I wasn't much tougher than they were to be able to withstand the cold, but experience had taught me that the discomfort only lasted so long. While the frigid temperature would feel like pins and needles when you were first submerged in the water, after a few minutes, it wasn't so bad. After ten minutes, you forgot that it was even cold to begin with. Our emotions are the same: if we can withstand the discomfort of nerves and anxiety in certain situations, over time, they fade away and the situation loses its power over us.* "

In 2014, many soccer fans were beginning to get concerned, especially those in Argentina. Their star player, Lionel Messi, had been seen throwing up on the soccer field in games leading up to the World Cup. Many people were worried he was sick and would not be able to perform at his best, and they needed him at his best. Messi wasn't just Argentina's star player, he was arguably the best player in the world, and the one who was going to lead Argentina back to World Cup glory.

Messi himself addressed the issue and explained, "I don't know what it is, but I had a thousand exams. I start to feel nauseous to a point where I almost vomit, and then it goes away." Despite his nausea, his performance was not hindered, as he sometimes scored within minutes of vomiting. Many people were puzzled, as even the team's medical staff was unable to find any physical reason or cause for his illness. Therefore, when questioned about it, Argentina's head soccer coach Alejandro Sabella attributed his star player's habit of throwing up on the field to nerves. One headline even revealed with surprise, "He's Human! Lionel Messi Is Sick Due to Nerves."[1]

The headline instantly caught my attention and caused me to roll my eyes. The media often displays shock and surprise at athletes who display any evidence of feelings. However, the assumption that athletes are superhuman stoics, which many may think is complimentary, is more problematic for athletes themselves than for anyone else. Headlines like the one about Messi's nerves seem to imply that those who compete and find success are expected to be infallible or, even worse, callous and emotionless, which sets an unattainable and unrealistic image. Nerves, for instance, become a sign of weakness or failure, rather than a sign of success. But being nervous means that you have something you value at stake.

More than anything else, being nervous is not a sign of failure but rather <u>a sign that you have made it somewhere worth being</u>.

Nerves are not the only emotion we have, and we all will experience a whole range of emotions, whether we are competing at the pinnacle of our sport around the world or living a simple small-town life. Sometimes you see the emotions in our actions, sometimes you hear the emotions in our words, and sometimes our bodies cause us to feel them in our upset stomach, tightening throat, or shaky legs—but not always, because we all process and display our emotions differently. But even though everyone's emotions manifest differently, and you may not always see or hear them, it does not mean we don't all experience them. The athlete on TV and even the rockstar on stage have both experienced every high and low that comes with those pressure-inducing moments. Being a professional doesn't make you immune to one of the most fundamental aspects of being human: emotions.

Lesson 13

EMOTIONS ARE ESSENTIAL

Regardless of how they manifest, our emotions are an essential part of the game and of life.[2] Many of us imagine being the best implies never having to doubt ourselves or have nerves present, but that is entirely untrue. Messi isn't alone at the top with his nerves and, more specifically, upset stomach. Olympic skier Mikaela Shiffrin threw up before her race at the 2018 Olympics, and legendary basketball player Bill Russell was known to throw up so much that his coach, equally legendary Red Auerbach, considered it lucky. However, after they expelled the contents of their stomach, all of them continued to perform. While Messi unfortunately didn't lead Argentina to World Cup glory, losing 1–0 to Germany in the championship game in 2014, all three of these athletes not only competed at the highest levels but solidified themselves as some of the greatest ever in their disciplines. They prove that success does not imply the absence of nerves, fear, or emotion in general. Success is executing your job even with them present.

While I was raised by a guy who was dubbed "the Ice Man" by local sports reporters, I always knew these emotions were fundamental to the process. I was fortunate enough to be able to see the things the media couldn't see from their press box and to have a more realistic perspective of the role emotions play in sports. To them, he is the coach who doesn't smile. The one who reveals nothing to anyone. Short in his responses to the press and tall in his orders to his team, I wouldn't be surprised if the press dreaded interviewing him as much as he dreaded answering their questions. However, I always found their impression of him hysterical because I knew it was only a small part of the story.

As a family, we openly discussed all those feelings, both good and bad. The excitement and joy, and the frustration and fears, were shared late at night at the kitchen counter after a game and on long car rides home. The stoic exterior didn't imply an avoidance or lack of emotion, just a different experience or display of them. He wasn't diminishing them by concealing them from the public, it was just his own natural disposition. He liked to keep his cards close to his hand and deliberately revealed them only to those who needed to see and only when they needed to see them.

While he may have been more silent, I always knew he valued and respected coaches on the other side of the spectrum, like his coaching colleague John Tortorella, an NHL coach who has been both praised and criticized for his public emotional outbursts on the bench and in press conferences. "Torts" is well known for his blunt and expletive-filled responses and rants, and my dad can't deny that he admires Torts's honesty and authenticity. Wearing his heart on his sleeve, Torts emotionally challenges his players with raw and honest feedback and doesn't hide from controversy in front of cameras. And even though it isn't always perceived in such a positive light, with media publishing articles with titles such as "John Tortorella and the 7 Angriest Coaches in the NHL Right Now," many of his players have defended his style.[3] Ryan McDonagh, who played for him with the New York Rangers, has said, "His emotion is there every single day. You've got to be prepared to match that and rise above it. You have to have a ton of respect for someone who has that much passion for the game. And he has your back as a player and as a team. He's not afraid to call other people out."[4]

Despite the support from many of his players and the success that he has had as a two-time Jack Adams Award winner for NHL coach of the year, his portrayal in the media is just another example of how emotion in performers and people in power is scrutinized far too often. Whether criticizing overly emotional displays of frustration and anger or questioning the ability of those who are nervous, headlines frequently highlight emotions as flaws. Throughout history, for instance, women specifically have been stereotyped and labeled as too emotional for leadership positions and unable to effectively make decisions. Those important jobs, people claimed, were not meant for emotions. However, what both the Ice Man and Torts know is that they not only experience emotions in their job but use them. As a coach and leader, you need to make important decisions, frequently with limited time and under extreme pressure. While many people may value reason and logic when it comes to decision making, emotion is equally if not more important—especially when we have little time to make those decisions.

In fact, there is evidence to suggest that without emotion we might not be able to decide anything at all.

In his book *Descartes' Error*, neuroscientist Antonio Damasio demonstrates the value of emotions through the story of his patient who suffered a brain tumor.[5] While his patient's intellect was completely unimpaired, his life seemingly began to fall apart. After numerous tests and analyses, Damasio made a remarkable discovery. His patient's emotional responses were virtually nonexistent. Damasio described his patient's reactions to emotionally charged images, and even to his own personal tragedy, as neutral. As a result, he was able to generate ideas to problems using his intelligence, but he struggled to choose an option. His lack of emotion limited his ability to evaluate his choices and effectively decide on anything. As Damasio writes, "Emotions and the feelings are not a luxury, they are a means of communicating our states of mind to others. But they are also a way of guiding our own judgments and decisions. Emotions bring the body into the loop of reason."

As we learn more about our brains, it has become clear that emotions provide us with insight and direction. We need them to guide us. In addition, they are critical when it comes to motivation and spurring movement in that right direction, especially in sports. That is why it isn't surprising to discover that the words *motivation* and *emotion* both come from the same Latin root, *motere*, which means "to move."[6]

If you eliminated all the emotion—the joy, fun, fear, and sadness—from sports, it would be difficult to understand anyone dedicating so much time and effort to these games. Imagine living in a world where no one felt disappointed in failure, nervous with opportunities, or fearful in the presence of a threat. Not much would happen in that world. No one would train or work hard to prepare, and as a result, no one would achieve much of anything. However, even though emotions are an integral part of our lives, many commentators are still surprised and a little disappointed when they learn that athletes are confronted with this very human experience on the playing field and in the arena.

Michael Jordan is a prime example of an athlete who knew how to use his emotions to propel himself to the highest level of achievement, but he also experienced the criticism one can receive for those emotions. Not only one of the most famous athletes of all time, Jordan was also one of the most dedicated and hardest-working athletes. He pushed both himself and those around him to become the very best they could be. However, he was oftentimes portrayed as a jerk for doing so, as the intensity of his emotions would come across as too much or unwarranted by spectators and even his peers. Many of these emotions stemmed from the disappointment and frustration he experienced when he was confronted with failure. It started when he got cut from his high school basketball team and continued to build with every lost game or championship he experienced throughout his career as he became what many people refer to as the greatest of all time.

Jordan became so self-aware of his own emotional drive that he would create reasons to evoke the emotions in himself necessary for him to perform at his best. For example, in 1993 the Washington Bullets traveled to Chicago to play Jordan and the Bulls. That night, a lesser-known player for the Bullets, LaBradford Smith, caught people's attention because he outscored Jordan in the game. Although Jordan's team won the game, being outplayed didn't sit well with Jordan. After the game, Jordan told his teammates that Smith had come up to him and said, "Nice game, Mike" as a subtle reference to their individual performances on the score sheet. As a response, the next night when they played each other again, Jordan went out and scored as many points as Smith did that whole first game in only the first half. In an interview given years later, however, Jordan admitted that Smith never made the comment and that he made it up as motivation. He evoked that anger and frustration that he knew fueled him.

Jordan's remarkable success and drive wouldn't have

happened without emotion. In 2009, when he was inducted into the hall of fame, Jordan gave a speech and said, "The game of basketball has been everything to me. My refuge. My place I've always gone when I needed to find comfort and peace. It's been a source of intense pain, and a source of most intense feelings of joy and satisfaction."[7] His experience highlights how those intense feelings are ingrained in every and any athletic experience, and are vital for achievement.

The takeaway here isn't what Jordan did, but how he did it. It was his level of self-awareness that allowed him to tap into the next level of his game. Jordan was not only aware of the power of his emotions, but, more importantly, had a profound understanding of himself. He knew how his different emotions influenced him and what triggered specific emotions in him. As a result, Jordan was able to manipulate his environment in a way that sparked his emotions to help him achieve his goals.

In order for you to reach your best, you need to know yourself first.

Each of us is an individual, and the solutions and strategies that worked for one athlete are not guaranteed to work for another. Every athlete has their own tendencies and their own process. You need to find what works for you, and sometimes that takes some trial and error as we learn more about who we are as people and as athletes. Then you can adjust things until you find a combination or approach that works for you.

I remember when my dad worked for the St. Louis Blues, and he used to tell me that Pierre Turgeon would wake up and go to the rink early on game days to do a heavy squat workout. Apparently, compared to all the extra weight in the morning, the workout made his legs feel light and free when he was on the ice later that night. Then I had friends in college tell me stories of other professional athletes they had heard of avoiding walking up or down stairs on game day to preserve their legs. Whether the second story is true or not doesn't really matter. The point is that there isn't one formula that works, and everyone is going to give you different advice. Take everyone's advice with appreciation, but don't feel the need to replicate their process. Many athletes could not perform at Turgeon's level regardless of their preparation, but for some, doing that workout would do the opposite of giving them an advantage.

As we work toward a greater understanding of ourselves and our needs, we can better develop a plan of action to prepare ourselves and navigate the many challenges we will face as we strive toward our individual goals. Given that our emotions are one of the fundamental components of our brain, they will undoubtedly be one of those challenges. Sometimes it may even feel as though they are our driving force, controlling us more than we like to admit. Yet those emotions are part of the reason I fell so in love with sports. Nothing in my life has made me more excited, happy, nervous, frustrated, or angry than the highs and lows of these games. It is intoxicating and brings you to life in a way that very few things in this world do. With such a powerful force, it is important for us to know how to use it. In the following sections, I will break down some of the reasons we struggle so much with our emotions and provide strategies that allow us to see how they can inform us, guide us, and motivate us, rather than allowing them to disrupt us.

Lesson 14

LIKE A MUSCLE
THE BRAIN NEEDS TIME
TO DEVELOP TOO

Using our emotions is easier said than done. The skills necessary for regulating our emotions in order to utilize them effectively reside in our prefrontal cortex, the rational decision-making center of our brain. Unlike our amygdala, which regulates our emotions and automatically responds to our surroundings, the prefrontal cortex is a bit slower and more effortful. If we were to be driven purely by our amygdala's powerful emotions, without our prefrontal cortex, our responses would be fast but sometimes regrettable. However, left to only our prefrontal cortex, without any emotion, we would have logic and reason without motivation or direction. When both our prefrontal cortex and our amygdala are in balance, we are able to obtain what emotional intelligence research refers to as self-mastery. Self-mastery is the combination of our awareness of our mental state and our ability to manage it, which is what sets apart outstanding individuals in any domain of performance.[8]

Unfortunately, our prefrontal cortex hasn't always been there to support us in this process. In fact, based on evolutionary psychology, our emotional brain developed long before our rational brain in our prefrontal cortex. Since our emotions can be triggered like reflexes, much quicker than any rational thought or logic, they were critical when responding to immediate danger and threats throughout history. These emotions, associated with the fight-or-flight response, protected us and kept us safe. However, as we continue to evolve and the world around us changes, these powerful and reactive emotions sometimes do more harm than good, leaving us to juggle that impulsive drive along with our newly developed, but slower, rational thought process.

This slower prefrontal cortex is the part of our brain that many people believe makes humans so special. Our ability to control and regulate emotions, to think rationally and logically, to predict consequences and control our impulses is what elevates our species above the rest. It is the part of our brain that takes those necessary and powerful emotions and implements them in a productive and effective manner. It transforms the raw emotion into those decisions and actions that are necessary for success.

Although we have evolved a great deal to elevate our species to this elite level, it comes at the cost of a slow developmental process. Unlike most species, which may be considered lucky to simply survive past twenty-five years, humans' brains are not even done developing until our mid-twenties—an age where some athletes are already retired from their professional careers. As a result of this maturation process, we have professionals not only earning millions of dollars but being scrutinized and criticized by millions of people around the world as they perform under extreme amounts of pressure, without fully developed brains in their heads. These professional athletes are held to the highest standards both on and off the athletic field without a mature frontal cortex to help them regulate and respond to the emotions often induced by those tense and high-stress situations. Maybe we should all consider that the next time we are typing a tweet or sharing some criticism of the latest athletic sensation.

In 2018, Swedish hockey player Lias Andersson faced the brunt of that criticism when he made headlines not for his play on the ice but for his reaction during the medal ceremony after the gold medal game at the World Juniors, the biggest hockey tournament for players under the age of twenty. Andersson, captain for team Sweden, had just earned a silver medal after suffering a heartbreaking loss to Canada in the finals of the tournament. After walking through the receiving line for his second-place award, Andersson promptly took off the silver medal that had been placed around his neck and tossed it into the crowd because he didn't want it. The reaction to Andersson's behavior was immediate, as there seemed to be more headlines, tweets, and comments about his silver medal toss than about Canada winning gold. People around the world were labeling the act as unsportsmanlike, immature, and unprofessional.

Despite his "unprofessional" behavior, this wasn't Andersson's first experience on the world stage. As a first-round draft pick, the nineteen-year-old had been representing Sweden on the ice for almost five years at that point. Over the course of that time, he had already acquired a bronze and two silver medals. In fact, this silver medal in 2018 was the third time Andersson experienced the heartbreak of losing in a gold medal game. That is a lot of disappointment for anyone, but especially someone who is experiencing that throughout the course of what would be his high school years.

As our frontal cortex is still developing, the intensity of the emotions we experience is much stronger. Without the fully formed prefrontal cortex to process those emotions, the power that they hold feels magnified. It is the reason why heartbreak, loss, disappointments, and fear all feel bigger when we are adolescents than later on in our adult life. It is also why adults often look at teenagers as if they are overdramatic.

Teenagers aren't overreacting; they are literally processing the experience differently in their brains.

Just a few months after his questionable behavior at the World Juniors, Andersson was representing Sweden again, this time at the World Championships with the senior national team. Finally, after all his heartbreak, Andersson was able to help secure a gold medal for Sweden and jokingly stated that he was not going to throw this one away.

Young and promising athletes are put on the world stage every day with high expectations and even tougher criticism. While their decision-making isn't fully developed or reliable at that point in their life, their emotions are firing at full capacity. This only compounds the trouble. All emotion with no logical thinking can result in some questionable and impulsive decisions. Add the context of an athletic event that triggers powerful emotions in even the most matured brain, and you have a recipe for emotional meltdowns in young athletes.

However, it is not just their behavior on the ice or playing field that is frequently criticized. Tyler Seguin, for instance, was portrayed as a problem for his occasional tardiness and poor decision-making off the ice when he played for the Boston Bruins in his early twenties. Common mistakes for someone his age—college aged—were put under a spotlight, leading many people to question his value and ability. This speculation even led to the *Boston Herald* labeling him a "problem child" when the Bruins eventually traded him away to Dallas in 2013. Years later, a *Sports Illustrated* article titled "Different Animal: How Tyler Seguin Has Evolved in Dallas" praised him for his mindset and leadership skills. However, Dallas didn't drastically change who Seguin was; they just had the benefit of time and the maturity that comes with that. At twenty-eight years old, Seguin was behaving differently than he did at eighteen when he joined the league and at twenty-one when Boston traded him and labeled him a problem rather than acknowledging what he truly was—a kid.

Sometimes, coaches, teachers, and parents of teenagers may feel as though they are living in two different realities. Even though they may look like adults and often act like them, they still have a lot of growing up to do physically inside their brains, a growth process that isn't visible from the outside. Just like you may adjust a physical exercise for someone who is still working on building their physical strength and stamina, offering additional support emotionally during this time can promote a more consistent performance all around. This may be as simple as checking in more frequently on their emotional state, allowing for more flexibility in the expectations for their emotional responses, and offering opportunities for them to express their emotions rather than trying to eliminate and control them. If you are a young athlete yourself, take the initiative to find a way to safely express and explore your emotions. Art, music, exercise, and journaling are all valuable outlets. In fact, studies have shown that journaling about both your emotions and your thoughts, particularly during traumatic or stressful experiences, can even lead to greater positive growth over time.[9]

As a coach working primarily with high school and collegiate athletes who are still developing those emotional skills and strategies, it has been a fundamental part of my job to provide guidance and support along the way. The emotions among this age group are ever present, and numerous times I have watched and listened as my athletes on the field or even my students in the classroom react with purely their emotions and not with logic or reason—saying and doing things that they later, once their amygdala has settled down and their frontal cortex is able to catch up, ultimately regret. The issue isn't whether they know right from wrong, but rather that they lack the ability to see it clearly in the heat of the moment. As a coach or teacher in these situations, responding to their emotions with more emotion doesn't help. The most impactful I have ever been as a coach and as a teacher is the times when I have given them time to cool off and allow their thoughts to catch up with the emotions that are firing off strong and fast.

One moment sticks out to me during my first year of teaching. I had a student sitting in my classroom whom I had been warned about before the year even started due to his attitude and disruptiveness in class. Over the first few months of the year, I thought the student and I had formed a good relationship, and he responded well in class when I had to reel him in from his antics. On this day, however, he wasn't just being disruptive, he was becoming rude to those around him. I could sense that something more was bothering him, as his short and mean comments were coming out with more emotion than he intended and clearly not stemming from the people the comments were directed at. Rather than make a scene or get angry, I just asked him to take a walk and come back when he felt as though he could be more respectful to those around him. He stomped out of the classroom while rolling his eyes.

He eventually returned, and the rest of the class went on without a disturbance. He even contributed to the group discussion positively before the class was over. At the end of class, I asked him to stay and chat with me for a minute, a conversation that I am sure he was dreading as he dragged his feet across the room toward my desk, assuming I was going to berate him for his attitude and behavior that day. Instead, however, I asked him if everything was OK. His face revealed his surprise as he struggled to answer the question.

In our conversation, I went on to acknowledge that we will all have bad days sometimes, and that is OK. I even admitted to him that if he had an attitude with me, while it wasn't acceptable, I could handle it and my feelings wouldn't be hurt. However, I could not allow, under any circumstance, him being rude and hurting the feelings of the other students in class. Then I offered him support if he wanted to talk about whatever was obviously bothering him. He politely declined and left.

More than twelve hours later, a little after midnight that night, I received an email from that same student, thanking me for taking the time to talk to him. I still have no idea what was bothering him that day, but I know that if I had judged him and criticized him like we do so many young adults for their emotional responses in situations, I would not have had the same result. In fact, I could have made the situation in my classroom worse that day not only for him but also for the other students who were affected by his comments.

More importantly, after that day, my student trusted me more than he ever did before. Instead of blaming him, I showed him that I was on his team and wanted to work with him rather than against him. As a result, he not only became more self-aware of his own emotions but came to me first when he was struggling with them. Then together we could find a way to cope with them that wouldn't disrupt or impact our class or the other students in it.

It doesn't always work to reason with emotion when emotion dominates our brains.

There is also no point in blaming an athlete, student, or person for their feelings and behavior when they aren't fully in control of them—this is true not just for adolescents, but all of us. Patience, understanding, and forgiveness are valuable things you can offer someone as a coach or teacher—or even to yourself in times of extreme emotional stress. Just like we know our muscles require repetition and time to develop, our brains' process of growth is no different.

Lesson 15

DON'T FIGHT THE CURRENT

When you are a coach, there will be daily instances when your athletes are struggling with their emotions. I have found that when I am working with a new team or athletes, they often come tell me when their emotions are particularly negative. For example, they will tell me, "I'm super frustrated," or, "I am really nervous." My first response in these situations is always a calm and accepting "OK." Frequently, however, my response is met with some confusion. Their faces convey the question, "Aren't you supposed to help me not feel this way?"

Over time, what my athletes realize is that when I ask them how they are feeling, or if they tell me unprompted, it is not a scale to measure success of some sort. It is simply a check-in. Feeling frustrated or nervous is OK. Moreover, acknowledging that emotion and naming it can help you regain some power and clarity as you navigate through the emotion, rather than attempting that exhausting task of fighting against it. When my athletes see me respond the same to their excitement as I do to their frustration or nerves or fear, they begin to realize that their emotion isn't the goal we are focused on. If I, as the coach, get sidetracked by their emotion and display disappointment in response to their negative emotions, I communicate a message that they are failing to achieve a certain standard or expectation. There

acknowledge your emotions. they are okay.

is no need to get upset about being upset. You can't always control the initial emotion; sometimes that is automatic.

The emotion is the reaction, and we want to focus on the response.

Let's consider overcoming mistakes, for example. This is one of the most emotionally driven challenges I focus on with athletes. Competitive and goal oriented, messing up or losing the ball or puck is extremely frustrating for them. Many athletes want to work with me to avoid that reaction of frustration. However, if they decide that they don't want to be frustrated in those moments and we set a goal focused on avoiding that emotional response, then we are setting them up for a downfall of dominoes.

The first domino to fall is the mistake. There is no doubt that this will happen eventually for any competitive athlete. It is part of the game. Because these athletes care and are competitive, the mistake will naturally evoke frustration— the second domino. As a coach, I want my athletes to care, and I want them to want to do well. The frustration after a mistake is much more promising than a lack of concern.

The third domino is all about choice. If we set our goal for our mental performance to be avoiding frustration, then not only will that domino fall as our goal is now unattainable, but it will also trigger more frustration and anger, collapsing all the dominoes in the row. Instead, if we decide to accept the frustration and set a goal focused on responding to the emotion, then that third domino doesn't fall but provides us with an opportunity to continue moving forward productively and stop the previously inevitable downfall.

Focusing on the response isn't always easy. While athletes initially want help trying to avoid the negative feelings they don't want to experience, I explain that avoidance is a waste of our valuable resources. If we spend our time trying to evade the emotions we don't want to feel, then our focus and energy aren't being directed toward executing the goals we are trying to achieve. The emotions are going to happen. That is a guarantee. Let's redirect our efforts toward the goals we are striving for but aren't guaranteed.

When we are in the middle of it, though, the power of our emotions can sometimes be as deep and strong as the ocean. I grew up on Cape Cod and spent a lot of time at the beach. Every summer, we would make sure we took time to go out to the National Seashore, where the water was much colder, but the waves were bigger than where we lived. The excitement of the waves, however, came at a cost. There was also the danger of an undertow, a strong current below the surface of the water. Now, undertows don't actually pull you under the water, but they do pull you out far from the shore. When you notice the beach getting farther and farther away, it can be pretty scary. People who get stuck in the currents can sometimes panic and spend all their energy trying to swim against the current and get back to the beach. Unfortunately, exhausting all their energy against a current much stronger than they are typically ends in defeat.

What you should do, if you ever find yourself caught in an undertow, is swim parallel to the shore. Not against the current, but just along it. Eventually, you will find yourself out of the current's strong pull and be able to easily swim to shore. This is very similar to "negative" emotions we experience in a game.

Emotions are simply a natural occurrence like an undertow. If we try to fight back, we just exhaust ourselves into defeat.

move w/ emotions, not against them.

Instead of going against them, if we can move with them, parallel to the shore, until we are out of the riptide of feelings, we will better be able to reach our intended destination.

In other words, rather than trying to eliminate emotions from our experience, I work with athletes to not only accept the emotions they will experience but to swim alongside them and regulate them more efficiently. Instead of letting the nerves or the fear hijack our performance, we want to integrate them into our process in a way that helps facilitate a favorable outcome. This isn't a simple fix, but acknowledging those emotions is a good first step. Being aware of our emotions and confronting them in a manner of acceptance and confidence, rather than avoidance, eliminates the power and control those emotions hold over you psychologically.

Once you are aware of your emotions, you can then label them.[10] Practicing labeling your emotions and naming them has been proven in research to increase both our understanding of them and our ability to regulate them more effectively. I often recommend that my athletes keep an emotion journal, a simple list of how they felt throughout the day and what they were doing when they felt each emotion. This then allows them to identify what causes certain emotions and prepare for when they may arise again. That way, instead of fighting the current, or emotion, they can set a goal focused on responding to the frustration, like swimming along the shore, that allows them to navigate the challenge with more success. This provides us with more effective coping mechanisms such as breathing, reappraisals, or clear action steps. (However, until our brains are fully developed, this all takes more effort and attention.)

The attempt to fight against the current of emotions can manifest itself in different ways. Sometimes it may be pure avoidance of an emotion, attempting to not feel a certain

label your emotions.

way, as I mentioned. Other times, it is the avoidance of the situation that causes the emotion—going through something as quickly as possible or not putting yourself in situations that will ultimately push you to become better because the pressure of that situation induces stress and anxiety that you would prefer not to feel. However, avoiding those situations doesn't reduce anxiety; it actually increases the power that situation has over you to produce greater anxiety in you in the future. In addition, your avoidance behaviors can negatively impact your ability to perform the task at hand.

An interesting example of this is demonstrated in the book *Twelve Yards: The Art and Psychology of the Perfect Penalty Kick* by Ben Lyttleton. The research in the book provides great insight to effective and ineffective emotional responses in a very specific game situation. Lyttleton reveals data that show those who took longer between the referee blowing the whistle and them shooting the ball during penalty kicks in soccer had a higher success rate. Those who rushed it missed more often. In other words, the quicker the athlete was to take the shot, the more driven they were by their nerves to just get the moment over with and get out of the uncomfortable situation.

From an operant conditioning perspective, which is just a form of learning through associations, this rushed behavior is rewarded through negative reinforcement. Negative reinforcement is when your behavior is directly correlated to the elimination of a negative stimulus and therefore more likely to reoccur. For example, if I offer my students a free homework pass for getting an A on their test, I am eliminating the undesirable homework and reinforcing the behavior of studying and preparing for the test. In the penalty kick scenario, taking the kick as soon as possible eliminates the feelings of stress and anxiety that were produced by the moment. Just like my athletes who wanted me to help them avoid feeling negative emotions, the athletes in Lyttleton's research responded in a way that allowed them to escape the negative emotion. Surprisingly to some, the reward of escaping the anxiety becomes more powerful than performing well. So, by focusing on avoiding or escaping that feeling, they did not focus on the task at hand, causing them to make more errors and miss the net more frequently.

Instead, the slower athletes were more accepting of their nerves and the pressure to linger a bit longer in the moment. Those extra few seconds allowed them to focus on their shot and technique. The composure to wait, despite the likely discomfort of their emotions in that moment, and respond with a deep breath seemed to be the key to success. As a result, the players with that poise under pressure were statistically more accurate at converting their penalty kick. While the current of our emotions in those tense moments can be strong, we don't have to fight against them to be successful. In fact, sometimes if we just sit with them for a moment, we realize their power is only momentary.

As I mentioned, the fun waves out on the National Seashore came at the cost of a strong undertow and extremely cold water. The temperature often discouraged many of my family and friends from getting in and enjoying the waves with me.

Emotions are like that cold water: they can be intimidating at first.

I wasn't much tougher than they were to be able to withstand the cold, but experience had taught me that the discomfort only lasted so long. While the frigid temperature would feel like pins and needles when you were first submerged in the water, after a few minutes, it wasn't so bad. After ten minutes, you forgot that it was even cold to begin with. Our emotions are the same: if we can withstand the discomfort of nerves and anxiety in certain situations, over time, they fade away and the situation loses its power over us.

In fact, this concept of facing the situations that evoke powerful emotions, instead of avoiding them, is the basis of the cognitive behavioral therapy technique of flooding.[11] In flooding, patients are exposed to prolonged exposure of stimuli that evoke high levels of anxiety and fear until the emotional and physiological responses associated with them have been greatly reduced. The reduction of anxiety simply comes as time passes and their inability to avoid the situation forces them to realize the stimuli are not as harmful as they imagined. While the initial exposure can increase fear due to the inability to escape, the overall experience has lasting effects on decreasing fear and anxiety.

As the years have progressed and I do more and more work with athletes on helping them accept and respond to their own emotions, I have noticed myself become more at peace with the turbulent feelings that can arise within myself throughout any day. I find nerves now give me more energy than butterflies, I have more patience with frustrating moments or challenges, and I address my anger in more solution-focused ways. I don't choose to avoid these situations, but instead embrace them. I relabel the butterflies in my stomach as a fire in my belly, something that will drive me and motivate me. I sit in the cold water of feelings until it settles, and I find my comfort zone expanding to include situations that once produced anxiety and fear.

Lesson 16

TALK THE TALK

Consider this advice: "Be happy," or "Don't be nervous." Has anyone ever said those things to you, or have you ever tried to say those things to yourself? If so, how successful were those statements at having the intended effect? Most likely, not very. When discussing emotions with the athletes I work with, the most important point I always try to make, and will repeat here numerous times, is that they happen. All the time. As I mentioned, my goal isn't to make you never feel nervous or frustrated or angry. In fact, if I did eliminate all those emotions, I think your experience playing the game you love would be greatly altered. We love playing games because of the emotions they give us, the good and bad. Without those downs, the ups wouldn't feel as intoxicating.

Those emotions are strong, but they are not the only thing your brain is capable of doing. Our brains produce emotions, but they also create thoughts and ideas and make decisions. Your brain is powerful, and for centuries, there have been philosophical debates over whether that power controls you or you control all that power. Now, we know that our emotions stem from the amygdala in the center of our brain, and while we can use them and work with them, we can't actually control them. Our thoughts, however, are typically thought to be more within our grasp. Those ideas flow through our cognitive awareness, personally crafted and chosen by us. As ancient philosopher René Descartes once said, [Except our own thoughts, there is nothing absolutely in our power.] However, despite Descartes's (and many of our own) beliefs, today there is a growing body of research that seems to suggest we don't even control those. Instead, both our thoughts and emotions are things that our subconscious conjures up without our conscious input at all. Therefore, we don't choose our thoughts or our emotions; we simply become aware of them.[12]

This concept of controlling the mind is strongly connected to a common misconception that many people have about mindfulness. People often want to discuss the growing trend of mindfulness and how challenging they find it—how they can't empty their mind and not think about anything, which is what they believe they are supposed to do in mindfulness practice. It is difficult because our brains weren't meant to be an empty void, and that isn't the purpose of mindfulness. If we did successfully empty that space completely, like a vacuum, our brain would quickly fill that emptiness with anything that is readily available (and that isn't always "good" things). That means when we try to think of nothing, we are ultimately handing the reins over to our brain to fill that space, and we surrender any little control we may have had.

Contrary to popular belief, mindfulness isn't total control; it is simply total awareness.

In fact, research has commonly defined it as paying attention with purpose—being in the moment and acknowledging the thoughts and feelings, both physical and intangible, that arise, rather than blocking them out or restricting them.[13] Once you notice a thought, you can let it pass and move on to the next thought. Awareness, however, does not imply control.

Most of our brains are like revolving doors, with thoughts continuously flowing in and out as new information or stimuli catch our attention. Sometimes they flow through so fast we miss them, unable to process them unless we are purposefully attending to the moment, which mindfulness encourages us to do. However, sometimes things get stuck in that revolving door like a trap, or a skipping record, constantly replaying the same word over and over again. The most common way for this trap to occur is to try to not think about something. *Don't mess up. Don't mess up. Don't mess up.* Like a small, barely noticeable pimple on the side of your face that you try to poke, prod, and squeeze to get rid of, a dangerous thought that we obsessively try to suppress and get rid of only becomes redder, swollen, and much more noticeable.

Guiding, rather than controlling, our thoughts is a more realistic approach to this challenge. In order to do this, one clever technique I use with my athletes is to take advantage of the few things we do control: our words and our actions. We all know we have much more control over our physical body than we do our internal mind. You may have all the feelings and thoughts that make you want to punch someone in the face, but it is much easier to withhold the punch than it is to suppress the feelings and thoughts associated with that desire. In addition, while we may think something, we don't always say it out loud. We have all proven throughout our lives that we can say and do things that do not reflect the thoughts and feelings we are currently experiencing.

When I work with athletes who are having trouble channeling their thoughts and emotions in the right direction, the first thing we check is their body language. Are they dropping their head and shoulders? Are they communicating to themselves and their opponent that they are defeated? Studies have shown that our body and actions can influence our emotions as much as our emotions can influence our body.[14] While we may not be able to tap directly into our brain to adjust our emotional state, we can manipulate our body to send signals to our brain to produce the desired feelings.

Stand tall when you feel unconfident. Smile when you feel nervous.

Have your actions reroute your thinking rather than your thoughts restricting your actions.

The second thing we analyze after their body language is their self-talk. While our thoughts may be passive, occurring without our control, our self-talk is proactive. It is what we are choosing to say to ourselves internally, and sometimes externally, and if we do it well, it can help us regain control and stay focused in those challenging moments. Our best defense against those negative thoughts that can fill our brain is to force them out with words that will help us, not hurt us. Sometimes it is optimistic and motivating, but often it is simply instructional. To construct that instructional self-talk, we begin by identifying what they want to do in that moment, and then we simplify it.

Typically, what the athletes I work with want to do is centered on their main outcome goal of winning, and the most challenging moments are ones that threaten the possibility of achieving that goal. Maybe the athlete feels as though they need to score (this all depends on the sport and position) and they aren't getting those chances or finishing them. If that is the case, then we simplify the elements of their game that lead to those scoring opportunities. What do you need to do on the field to give yourself the chance to score a goal, and what do you need to do to make the most of that chance? For most team-sport athletes, the game boils down to movement, passing, battling, and the technique of their shot. You can't win the game in the first minute, but you can win that fifty-fifty ball. You can find the open pass and move. You can focus on your follow-through. If you can busy yourself and your mind with self-talk that is focused on what you need to do, then you are unable to dwell on the negative emotion or distracting thought that was previously sidetracking you.

While the answer to that question—what do you need to do to create scoring chances?—may be obvious to my athletes as we discuss it or even to you as you read it in this book, it is still important to identify those key things before those challenging moments come up in games.

Don't leave it up to chance that you will think of the "right" things at the right times.

When we are already physically tired and emotionally drained in the middle of a game, our brains will not be able to find the best response so effortlessly. Instead, if you identify what you want to say to yourself and prepare those responses like a script, it will help you feel more in control of the moment and require less energy from you mentally.

Consider the following: if I ask you what two plus two is right now, you probably have the answer before you even finish reading this sentence. Now imagine being asked the same question in the middle of an overtime game after facing ten consecutive shots as a goalie, or the second you cross the finish line after running in a five-mile race—your first response in those moments may be, "What?" as you try to catch your breath enough to speak. You can't as effortlessly process the question when your mind and body are busy taking care of your physical needs and processing all the other incoming information. It is a question you know the answer to, but if you aren't prepared to answer that question in that moment, then it becomes much more difficult. Even if you can answer it in a second or two, once your brain is able to catch up, those seconds that you waste can make all the difference in your performance. However, if I told you before the game or before the race that I was going to ask you what two plus two is at the end, you wouldn't need to think; you would have the answer ready as soon as the question was asked. The same is true for our self-talk. We know what we want to be saying to ourselves, and we know what we should be thinking. But if we are not prepared to respond to those challenges in the moment, then shifting ourselves back on track and regaining that "control" becomes much more difficult.

I tested the impact of instructional self-talk on performance when I was working at a sports vision clinic, training athletes' cognitive performance. In sports, where there are multiple moving pieces, unpredictable changes, small targets, and split-second decision-making, an athlete's eyes are critical to their performance. Where I worked, I was training athletes to take that information in visually and then process it faster and more effectively. In other words, I wanted athletes to be able to see more of the game and make more informed decisions. As Braden Holtby, an NHL goaltender who has been a longtime supporter of vision training, has been quoted saying in numerous articles, "If you're not seeing it, nothing else matters. Your eyes are the basis of your whole game."

In the simplest terms, sports vision training improves

your visual processing speed and, as a result, your reaction time and decision-making under pressure. However, it is more than just that. It is complete cognitive training that improves information processing, focus, and mental toughness. I spent most of my time figuring out how to mentally challenge and overload athletes—testing their limits, presenting them with drills involving excess stimuli, and forcing them to juggle (literally and mentally) numerous tasks and objects while shifting their attention and making decisions.

The drills were stress inducing for the athletes and made mental performance not only tangible but visible. You could physically see signs of frustration and anxiety. You could hear the thoughts in the athlete's head as they verbalized them out loud, sometimes to me specifically but oftentimes to themselves as they muttered under their breath (or screamed it out loud). You could even see the impact these thoughts had on performance, as you could pinpoint the exact moments they began to struggle or feel overwhelmed. It was the greatest sport psychology experimental setting I had ever been in. I could control the environment, I could manipulate the stimuli, and I could compare data, both quantitative (reaction time, performance scores, etc.) and qualitative (athlete feedback).

It was here that I began a new approach, not just with athletes at the clinic, but with all the athletes who reached out to me as a mental skills coach for my own business. Every single athlete I worked with, I taught how to juggle. It was a simple progression, and most athletes learned within a day or two. Once they mastered it, I added more cognitive challenges to it. At the most basic level, though, the learning process was simply a visible demonstration to athletes who were new to the world of sport psychology how their thoughts, and more importantly their <u>words, could</u> impact their <u>performance.</u>

"Start with two balls. Toss, toss, catch, catch. Literally talk yourself through it out loud. Give yourself instructions. Toss, toss, catch, catch."

 <u>When you tell yourself what to do next, you fill your mind</u> with that task. Rather than trying to not think something like, *"Don't drop it. Don't drop it. Don't drop it . . ."* your brain is busy telling yourself what to do next. *Toss it. Catch it.* Now it gets more complicated when you get to three balls. Telling yourself each step would be too much. *"Toss. Catch. Toss. Catch. Toss. Catch. Toss. Catch . . ."* While the words themselves aren't a lot, being able to keep up with the speed at which you toss and catch can result in your mind getting a bit flustered. So, we simplify it.

"OK, so with three balls you are going to throw in the exact same pattern as you did with two. As you go, just talk yourself through it: toss, toss, toss, toss . . ."

Why do I focus on the word toss and not the word catch? Well, the <u>catching is the part most people worry about,</u> but that is the second step, not the first. If a soccer player shoots the ball and is worried she is going to miss the net as she is shooting, then she is more likely to miss the net. She is worried about the outcome and therefore thinking too far into the future. Instead, she needs to <u>focus on the process of shooting,</u> maybe her foot placement or her stride. When you are juggling, if you are worried about catching all the balls, then you aren't focusing on tossing the balls. As a result, the toss ends up being less controlled, making the catch more difficult to do. If you focus on giving yourself a good, consistent toss, the catching part is easy. Don't skip steps. Focus on the first things first.

"Talk yourself through it out loud. If you don't want to say 'toss,' you can count each toss instead. One, two, three, four . . ."

At first, many athletes feel awkward talking themselves through it out loud. They may be giving themselves directions internally, but they don't want to verbalize it so other people can hear. However, we know we don't always have complete control of our thoughts, and the nervous thoughts like, *"Oh crap I almost dropped that," "Don't miss this one,"* can still sneak in between each *"toss."* When you say it out loud, not only are you intentionally filling that space in your mind so nothing else can creep in, but it is now also reinforced three times over.

You think it. You say it. You hear it.

The power of those words is suddenly magnified, and it is more likely to drown out and overpower any other internal thoughts.

One of my favorite YouTube videos is on this self-talk process produced by NFL Films.[15] In addition to discussing the power and benefits of self-talk, they provide clips of NFL players who were mic'd up and demonstrate external, or verbal, self-talk. You get to hear the kinds of things these players are saying to themselves, out loud on the field. Just like I encouraged my athletes to tell themselves out loud to toss the ball, these professional athletes are telling themselves, out loud, what they want to do. I think it is one of the coolest things ever because it provides us a glimpse into their mental strategy.

Many of the things they say in the video are not profound. They are not reciting poetry or revealing groundbreaking secrets about football performance. Some focus on motivational self-talk, telling themselves they are fast and strong and great. Some focus on task-oriented self-talk, telling themselves to see the ball and move their feet. While they each are telling themselves something different, they all are consistent, repetitive, and out loud. Many of the players repeat the same two or three words over and over again, making sure they fill that space and don't leave a vacuum to suck up any wandering thoughts or loose ideas.

The best self-talk script, I tell my athletes, is one that is like that annoying song you can't get out of your head. It is repetitive. It is catchy. And it pops into your head and just stays there on repeat, allowing you to hum along while performing other tasks. Sometimes, you don't even notice you're singing along. However, there will always be moments that our emotions and our brains take over and we feel like we are caught in an undertow that is too strong for us to survive. When that happens, we need to fall back on the things we do control. That is why I always remind my athletes the fundamentals of managing their emotions—having strong ABS: acceptance, body language, and self-talk.

Accept that emotions will happen, so when they arise it is neither surprising nor startling.

Focus on controlling your body so it reflects how you want to feel and what you want to do. And finally, talk the talk by intentionally filling that space in your head with the words you want and need to hear.

Lesson 17

LOOK FOR WHAT YOU WANT

As an athlete, when things become challenging, it suddenly becomes easy to spot all the mistakes or roadblocks on your way to success. When all you want is a win, sometimes the victories are hard to find. However, they are always there. They just may not be as big as we want them to be. We may not be winning the game or scoring the goal, but in every situation, there are wins worth celebrating and things to be grateful for. But unless we are looking for them, we won't see them.

When those challenges arise, a coach or leader's job is to help their athletes find what they need. Highlight those small wins and identify some solutions to the problems they are facing. Your team may not be playing great, but what is working and how are you going to build on that?

Anyone looking for an excuse can find one. Anyone looking for a problem can find multiple.

True positivity doesn't mean that you don't see the difficulties or challenges in the road ahead. It doesn't mean you are oblivious or ignorant to the obstacles or even losses you may face or mistakes you are making. What it does mean is that, instead of dwelling on those facts, you are willing to focus on finding solutions and benefits. Furthermore, even on those hardest days, you believe in your ability to get through it and have faith that better days will come.

Preaching absolute optimism and blind positivity in a team setting can be detrimental because it invalidates the feelings that your athletes are undoubtedly going to experience, and it overlooks the profound value that exists within that struggle. Furthermore, it perpetuates that dangerous culture or belief that your effort and struggle are something to be ashamed of rather than admired and praised. However, acknowledging struggle, commending effort, and highlighting the good and possible solutions among those challenges is your job as a coach.

Now, finding the good in the bad and building a positive mindset takes more work and self-awareness than some of us realize. That critical amygdala of ours is emotional, but also very negative. It is designed to find those "worst-case scenarios" and identify possible dangers and threats in the world around us to keep us safe. As a result, it is no wonder that our habitual response is to focus on the bad rather than the good so we can protect ourselves from it.

This negativity bias that is ingrained in all humans explains why minor or momentary failures can lead to a cycle of losing that is difficult to escape.[16] When we struggle to see the good moments in unfavorable outcomes, we may feel hopeless even when there is plenty of evidence to suggest otherwise. As a result, even small setbacks or mistakes become amplified and have a far greater impact on our psyches than the many positive moments that exist in that space.

It is undeniable that we are creatures of negative habit, and simply resisting that negative reflex can be difficult. Like most habits, this occurs without our conscious awareness. Actions like biting our nails or twirling our hair are formed over time, until they become so ingrained in our behavior that we don't notice ourselves doing them. However, just because habits can form subconsciously doesn't mean we can't make conscious decisions to counteract them.

The task to overcome a bad habit is not an easy one, though. Anyone who has ever had to quit a bad habit, like smoking or biting their nails, will tell you that it is much easier said than done. The stubbornness of the behavior stems from the reward system in our brain that feeds off the endorphins, the high, the decrease in stress, or whatever outcome is produced by the behavior and thus hardwires the action into an automatic response. As a result, you can't keep yourself from doing it before you're doing it. Suddenly, you find yourself with a cigarette in hand, or nails in your mouth, as the habit slipped back in undetected until it was too late. Therefore, resisting the urge is effortful, tiring, and sometimes feels near impossible.

However, with some discipline and awareness, we can rewire that brain of ours.

The trick isn't to suppress the undesired behavior, but instead to replace it with a more productive one.

As Timothy Gallwey explains in *The Inner Game of Tennis*, "In short, there is no need to fight old habits. Start new ones. It is the resisting of an old habit that puts you in that trench. Starting a new pattern is easy when done with a childlike disregard for imagined difficulties."[17] Don't focus so much time or energy on what you don't want to do, and just shift to what you can do instead. We have proof that habits are hard to break, so why not make habits that we want to last and have those become stronger than the bad ones?

Rather than trying to avoid dwelling on the bad, focusing on the good is a habit that we can form to replace our negative tendencies with some time and effort. When it comes to that realistic optimism, it may be unnatural for us at first. However, if we practice it enough, we can train ourselves to see the good as automatically as we bite our nails or twirl our hair. It is the same way we train certain skills on the field.

For example, every soccer player has a dominant foot. It is the one that feels more natural when you kick the ball and more in control when you trap it. To be honest, the other foot can sometimes feel utterly useless and uncoordinated. As a result, you form a habit to favor your dominant foot and instantly react on the field to adjust your body to use that foot even if the nondominant foot would be a better option. It becomes a reflex that happens without you even thinking about it. If I were to one day consciously try to resist the urge and stop using my dominant foot in a game scenario where my nondominant foot would be a better option, my play would be awkward, slow, and ineffective. However, if I instead dedicated time and repetition to practice using my nondominant foot, the communication in my brain would become smoother and faster, and the behavior over time would become just as automatic as my dominant foot's.

Stop focusing on the negative? Well, it's not so easy either—it is just as hard as avoiding your dominant foot on the soccer field. That is why we want to practice finding good things around us instead. Let's train our brains to make optimism our subconscious and automatic response in all types of situations. The best way to make this shift is to build a habit of gratitude. Taking time to identify the things you are grateful for, even in the most difficult moments, is a powerful practice.[18] In fact, research has shown that an intentional gratitude practice in college students increased their focus both in and outside of the classroom and helped them sustain their effort in the face of academic challenges.[19] This gratitude not only leads to greater outcomes but also demonstrates an increased resiliency. However, practice is truly the key word in the phrase "powerful practice," because gratitude requires much of it.

Becoming more optimistic and grateful isn't a simple transition.

In order to reap the benefits of gratitude, we require deliberate practice, just like any physical skill. Writing things down, big or small, may at first feel forced for some people. However, if you stay committed to it, over time, looking for and finding things to be grateful for isn't effortful and becomes more like second nature. More importantly, research on gratitude has demonstrated that this practice has the ability to increase sport satisfaction in athletes and decrease both distress and burnout.[20]

Whether you are a coach talking to your team at halftime, an athlete analyzing your own performance, or a human just navigating the daily hardships and challenges in life, if you want to have a better outlook, then you have to begin by consciously looking for the positives. If you don't make a conscious effort to look for the good, you might miss it even when it is all around you. I realized how much around us goes unnoticed when I was introduced to a new game as a kid. The game challenged you to be the first person on long car rides to spot a car with one headlight out. I was skeptical when the game was explained to me that we would find even one car, but before I knew it, we had spotted numerous. I was amazed at how I hadn't noticed how common it was for a car's headlight to be out until my attention was shifted to searching for it. Like most things you do as a kid, the game eventually faded from an essential for every car ride to simply a memory of the past. However, more than just the memory lingers; it is also a new habit. Ever since playing that game, my eyes always glance over and make note when I pass a car with a headlight out.

Lesson 18

BE THE CALM IN THE STORM
BE THE STORM IN THE CALM

When I entered graduate school, I knew I wanted to focus my research on coaching. More specifically, I was interested in the coaching moments that combine powerful emotions with little control—game time. While coaches can control most of their environment all week in practice, planning every detail down to the minute, come game time, they have to surrender their power and hope they prepared their team to the best of their ability.

The pregame speech is one of the last moments before the game starts that a coach can prepare for and plan ahead of time. After the whistle blows, no one knows for sure what will happen. Therefore, for my master's thesis I wanted to examine those moments where coaches must read and respond to situations in the moment. I chose to focus on one of the few moments in a game where coaches regain control but are given very little time to prepare—the intermission. What did they say, what did they do, what changes did they make? But more importantly, why and how did they make those decisions?

My research was focused on this small window where coaches hope to make a big impact. In movies, they flip over tables and give heart-wrenching speeches.[21] They tell their athletes that a bruise on the leg is a hell of a long way from the heart. The reality, I learned, is less dramatic and more practical. But that doesn't mean they don't feel the desire to flip a few tables, as one coach admitted to me. The emotions in the locker room of both the coaches and the players became one of the most prominent features of my research that dictated much of the coaching decisions in those pivotal moments of competition. More specifically, I found the coaches who were the most successful demonstrated the four key elements of emotional intelligence: self-awareness, self-management, social awareness, and relationship management. We have examined self-awareness and self-management quite a bit already, but now we are going to see how understanding other people's feelings, social awareness, how to respond, and relationship management is also a crucial components of performance, especially in team settings.

There are endless challenges when it comes to both sports and life. In a game, sometimes those challenges are tactical and may require adjustments in your strategy or approach. However, oftentimes those challenges are internal, managing the intense emotions that arise in us all. In team settings, it is not just your own emotions that are impacting the success and outcome of your performance but the emotions of everyone around you. Teammates and coaches have a significant impact on one another, and the ensuing emotional tug-of-war can be detrimental if not managed appropriately.

Within those team environments, a great leader is someone who is able to understand the emotional needs of those around them and fulfill those needs, regardless of their own emotional state. As one of the coaches I interviewed for my research explained,

"It is not how you feel that matters in the moment; it is what your athletes need that matters."

However, identifying what others need is not always an easy task. Therefore, one of the best places to start is to offer balance. Don't tip the scale by mirroring how they feel, but bring them back to neutral, where they can focus on the task at hand.

When things are not going great and your athletes, students, employees, teammates, or anyone you are trying to lead are experiencing emotions that are strong and turbulent, you may be tempted to share those feelings. In fact, chances are you do. However, while we know that we can't control how we feel, we can control what we do and what we say in response to that emotion. More often than not, displaying your negative emotions as a leader will only add to the turmoil of the moment. If your goal is to redirect your athletes away from their frustration and anger to something more productive, responding with frustration will not help guide them there. Instead, all you are doing is reaffirming their current mood.

Rather than mirroring their emotions, try setting a different type of tone. Instead of getting loud to overpower their emotions, try being calm and quiet. If you speak softly, you will force them to dial in and settle down, to really listen and hear you. Make them focus on you, not the emotion or the challenge at hand. On the other hand, when your athletes are quiet, maybe due to a lack of energy or confidence, you should bring the noise. Turn up the dial for them when they can't. The best description of this came from Cornell hockey coach Mike Schafer when he explained to me, "I try to be quiet in the eye of the storm . . . and be the storm when it's quiet."

"Be the calm in the storm" has been a motto I have tried to live by as a coach ever since then. Every coach has experienced the storm, and every coach has experienced the quiet.

The storm can be overwhelming, and the quiet can be intimidating.

Having a clear role defined for myself in those emotionally tense moments has allowed me to navigate them with more confidence and clarity.

According to emotional intelligence research, the emotional subtext in our interactions can be more powerful than the actual content of what we communicate. In other words, the tone of your voice has been shown to have a greater bearing on the outcome of the interaction than the actual things we say. A study done by researcher Marie Dasborough demonstrated this by examining the emotional states of two groups after receiving feedback.[22] One group received negative feedback with positive emotional signals, such as smiling and nodding, while the other group received positive feedback with negative emotional signals, such as frowns and furrowed brows. Although the second group received more positive feedback, they felt worse about their performance than the group who received negative feedback with positive emotional signs, highlighting that the emotional delivery of the message was more impactful than the content of the message.

Those emotions are both informative and contagious in a group setting. Typically, it is the most emotionally expressive person who sets the tone for the group—the one who is the loudest and most dramatic. However, in contexts where there are power differences, it is the most powerful person in the room who sets the emotional tone for those around them, like a coach or a captain in a locker room.[23] This means the leader's response and reaction to others' emotional states is critical to the team's overall state and mindset.

As a leader of any type, it can be difficult to get a feel for what your team needs in every moment. To further complicate the challenge, every individual on the team may need something different. When it comes to arousal and emotion, we all have our sweet spot where we perform best. For a coach in an emotionally charged locker room, you have to try to get everyone to their sweet spot.

According to the Yerkes-Dodson law, often referred to as the Inverted-U Theory, arousal increases our performance, up until a certain point, and then our performance begins to decline. If our arousal is too low, we are bored or uninterested, resulting in silly mistakes or lack of effort. If our arousal is too high, we are anxious and stressed, unable to execute. Like Goldilocks and the three bears, somewhere in the middle is just right. However, the middle sweet spot has a range. Some people perform better on the lower end of arousal, leaning more toward calm and steady. Other people perform best with a high level of arousal, feeling amped and energized.

Reflecting on some of your best performances as an athlete and how you felt in those moments can help you identify what your ideal zone may be. Did you feel calm and steady, or were you buzzing with energy? Then you can try to implement routines, including specific music, self-talk, and actions that can facilitate that level of arousal. However, regardless of where each player needs to be, as a coach, you need to try to steer your team away from the extremes on either end.

Phil Jackson, who has won eleven NBA titles as a coach, is a guy who values emotional intelligence before many others in his field, and he knows the importance of being in the right zone to perform. Introducing mindfulness to his teams and building it into his own coaching philosophy, Jackson was able to use his insight to navigate the chaos and emotion during games to help his team find success. One of the players who benefited from Jackson's coaching with the Chicago Bulls was Dennis Rodman. Rodman, as we discussed in the previous section, was a challenging player who brought many of his unique qualities to the court and had a tendency to sometimes get lost outside of his ideal performance zone. Jackson was aware of this and managed his own emotions in a way to positively influence Rodman. "I had watched [Rodman] before when he was with the Detroit Pistons," Jackson explained.[24] "And Chuck Daly, who I admired as a coach, was an animated coach. And as he got animated Dennis would become more animated on the court. Like his energy source was right there feeding into Dennis's energy source. So, I thought [Rodman] sometimes can go over the edge. I better just sit back and become quiet. And use [my] meditation practice as I am sitting on the bench."

If the team or a player isn't in the correct emotional or arousal state to perform, it is the coach's job to get them there. Balance them out and get back to that sweet spot in the middle. That requires the insight to be able to identify where the players are emotionally and where they need to be. In addition, it requires the coach to understand their own emotions and manage them in a way to project to the team whatever it is they need. This juggling act of self-awareness, interpersonal awareness, and self-control is the ultimate test of emotional intelligence.

Too often, teams in a panic will toss out their game plan

and try to achieve success by doing something completely different.

For the coach who is steering the ship, staying calm sets the tone for the rest of the crew to follow and provides them with stability in moments of chaos.

As a coach myself, I have tried to implement this. There are many times I have seen my own teams get worked up almost to a frenzied state of panic when they get frustrated on the field. Standing on the sidelines, my frustration builds up as well. I am losing patience with their careless mistakes and angry at their lack of composure. However, I can sense that increasing their stress and arousal by coming down on them about their errors isn't what they need. They are already caught up in a storm of emotions, swirling around on the field like a tornado with no direction. Instead, helping them navigate the storm by being calm and finding solutions, rather than pointing out errors, is always more effective.

"How do we feel?" I ask as they settle down in our half-time huddle, the negativity radiating off them. They hesitate to share their responses out of fear that I will come down harder on them. Eventually, a few players speak up and we come to the conclusion that things aren't great. I agree, calmly and without a trace of frustration in my voice. It's just a fact—we aren't playing well. They should be frustrated, I tell them. They are better than this. Then we move on to try and figure out why things aren't working. What can we do differently to have a better second half? Usually, that requires getting back to the key elements of our game rather than trying to overcompensate and do something different or new.

Lesson 19

BE POSITIVE BUT HONEST

While how you deliver a message is important and being calm in the storm is a good rule of thumb, what you say does matter if you want to help people achieve their goals. The challenge of what you should say in difficult moments came up one morning when I was sitting at the kitchen counter with my dad—another breakfast talk, but this time I was able to add more insight than just my distaste for Jaromír Jágr. I remember him standing by the stove as we were reflecting on our own experiences as athletes with various coaches. He was sharing a story about a time when he was a student athlete and his teammates were upset with the way their coach had handled an intermission. They were playing poorly, and I guess their coach told them exactly how he felt about their performance in a very animated way. This response left some of his teammates disgruntled and frustrated. My dad looked at me with his hands up—*What did they expect him to come into the locker room and lie to us?* His job, my dad tried to explain, was to tell them how they were doing, not make up something that wasn't true. They were playing poorly; it was simply a fact. He wasn't wrong, but I smiled and responded, "Well, isn't a coach's job technically to give your team whatever they need at that moment, not just what they think? In that moment, that obviously wasn't what they needed."

His head kind of nodded in agreement. "Fair point," he

said and sighed. It was a fair point, but not a clear solution. As we both knew, knowing what your team needs at any given moment isn't easy. Every coach has said the wrong thing and done the wrong thing in an attempt to give their team the right thing—that "whatever" it is that they need. It isn't a math problem with a clear answer, but a puzzle that is always missing some pieces.

To gain more insight into this puzzle, we can learn things from those who have found success. Although psychology traditionally grew out of the study of disordered and destructive behavior, some newer perspectives started to realize the value of focusing on the successful behaviors. Why not study the outliers who achieved great things? At the core of this change was humanistic psychology, which centers its main goal on helping people reach their full potential, a goal any athlete or coach is striving to achieve. Carl Rogers, one of the founding psychologists of this perspective, identified three key features of a growth-promoting culture that helps people reach this ultimate or ideal version of themselves: empathy, genuineness, and acceptance.

Empathy, or sensing what others are thinking and feeling, is at the core of emotional intelligence, as we discussed. The next step of emotional intelligence is knowing what to do with that information and how to respond to those thoughts and feelings. Many times, a coach can sense that an athlete or team is frustrated or distraught but not know what to say that will help achieve the outcomes they are hoping for—feelings of confidence, determination, and motivation.

The obvious and accurate response would be to stay positive. As one coach in my thesis research exclaimed, "Every time that I've come back from large deficits, I have been positive in the locker room. I have come back and won games from being down 4–0 and 3–0. Every time we've done that

I've gone in after that first period and been really positive." However, positivity alone won't fix every challenge at hand. Positivity, while rooted in optimism, is most effective when connected to reality. An honest analysis of the current situation provides more guidance and motivation than blind optimism that doesn't reflect the true challenges at hand.

Positivity is hopeful but not naïve.

This is where Carl Rogers's theory and the other two elements of his growth-promoting culture, genuineness and acceptance, provide valuable insight. Genuineness refers to being open with one's true thoughts and feelings, and acceptance is feeling totally welcome despite your faults. In my opinion, genuineness and acceptance are critical in taking your empathy to the next level and effectively navigating emotional contexts with others, like those we experience in athletic competitions and life in general.

Anytime I give feedback to an athlete, team, or student, I know I need to be honest with them. If I prioritize positivity over honesty, then my feedback will come across as disingenuous and demotivating. However, when I deliver that honest, but often critical, feedback, I also need to be accepting of them—make it clear that I still believe and support them despite the mistakes or flaws that are present in their performance. I am their coach. They are my team. Through good and bad, we will win, lose, fail, and succeed together.

My dad made a good point in the story I shared about when he asked his upset teammates back in his playing days if they expected their coach to lie to them when they were playing awfully. If they did expect that, then he wouldn't have been a very good coach. Yes, a coach's job is to give the team whatever they need in that moment—and it most likely isn't brutally honest and negative feedback—but a good coach also pushes his players and doesn't let them settle for less than they are capable of. A good coach is honest.

It isn't helpful for a coach or anyone offering feedback or analysis to not address the facts, even if those facts are that you are losing and are not executing things at your capable level. If we are going to have any chance of turning the situation around and improving it, we need to acknowledge that improvement needs to happen and that it is possible—emphasize that there is in fact room for improvement. If I tell you that you are doing your best when you are not, I immediately cap your performance at its current level.

Furthermore, an inaccurate evaluation of the current situation can invalidate the experience of those you are trying to work with. We know how valuable emotions are, and to disregard them as frivolous—or worse, misguided—will not magically eliminate them and produce the desirable positive emotions you are searching for. Instead, it can leave individuals in a confused state of guilt and shame for their feelings and without a realistic plan to move forward.

A 2002 study examining communication between health care professionals and their patients demonstrated this importance of honesty and realistic appraisals.[25] The study found that in an attempt to protect patients from potentially devastating or upsetting news, many doctors did not provide clear and honest information to their patients about their symptoms, diagnosis, and treatment. Unfortunately, this approach actually created greater challenges for their patients rather than relieving them of excessive hardships. In fact, the lack of honesty and truth in the information provided to the patients, meant to spare them the harsh reality of their prognosis, typically resulted in an increase in fear, anxiety, and confusion. Furthermore, it robbed them of the opportunity to adjust, prepare, and set more attainable goals.

I too noticed this tendency to lean too heavily on optimism and some of its adverse effects during the coronavirus pandemic. Back at school, with all our restrictions in place and opportunities fading away from many of our students, they were struggling to stay positive. Moments they had looked forward to for years and plans they had anticipated falling into place were suddenly stolen from them, for no reason other than bad timing. Had they been a year older, things would have been normal. It wasn't fair. In response to this, many of the adult members in our community doubled down on their optimism, even though they were admittedly struggling themselves to cope with the burden of the pandemic behind closed doors. "Be grateful you are in school!" they reminded students daily, along with an emphasis on how fortunate we were and how good we had it.

As a result of the optimism from many of the adults who overlooked the numerous challenges and losses, the students frequently felt more ostracized from the people who were meant to provide them with support. Teachers and administrators, who should be the ones to help students set goals, both academically and personally, displayed frustration with the disappointed and discouraged teenagers. Communication broke down as many students felt unheard, and motivation dwindled.

As I mentioned in Lesson #3, things happen, and the only thing you can do is the next one. Lying to yourself or to others about the reality of a situation doesn't help you handle those situations any better. In fact, it makes it more difficult to identify the next thing you can do. Contrary to popular belief, a positive mindset isn't thinking that everything is great. Trying to convince yourself and others that everything is great or perfect when it isn't does more damage than good over time. Just like suppressing our emotions, lying to ourselves and others about the reality of a situation becomes exhausting and impossible to sustain.

So, if a positive approach isn't telling your athletes that everything is great, what does positivity look like and sound like? What does it mean to positively see the empty half of the glass, and not negatively ruminate on it? True positivity is acknowledging the difficult days, the challenging moments, and the crappy circumstances and knowing you can get through them. It stems from the clichéd, but true, controllables we already discussed.

The power lies in the decisions you are making, the actions you are taking, and the perspective you are choosing.

In fact, if you feel the need to think that everything is good all the time, then you most likely don't have the confidence that you can get through the difficult times.

I often relate a positive mindset to Carol Dweck's growth mindset.[26] Individuals with a growth mindset are driven by a belief system that they can always improve. The tiny, but powerful, word *yet*. I can't do that . . . yet. A growth mindset is not an unrealistic perspective of the moment. It isn't a distorted or inflated sense of confidence in your current ability to do a certain task. It isn't saying you can do all these things right now. Instead, a growth mindset simply believes in the possibility of the future, and the value of time, practice, and determination. At one point in time, every single NHL player couldn't skate and every MLB player couldn't catch. Things you can't do now are simply things you can't do yet.

To help athletes implement a true positive mindset, I take

advantage of another three-letter word: *but*. Yes, the glass is half empty . . . *but* what can we do about it, what are we still grateful for, and what can we gain because of that now vacant space? Correcting athletes—or worse, reprimanding them—when they are voicing frustrations and honestly expressing their feelings won't eliminate those thoughts; it will just make them invisible (or inaudible) to you. Helping athletes continue their expression with a *but* teaches a more accurate sense of positivity in a challenging context. It marries the concepts of positivity and honesty in the reality you find yourself in.

In my graduate school research, while positivity was always expected as a critical component of coaching, honesty was one of the other most consistent findings across all coaches. "You can't go in there and bullshit them," as one coach told me. When your team isn't playing great, your team is usually the first to know it. Going in the locker room and telling them the opposite doesn't magically change that. However, adding a *but* to the end of that truth shifts the focus from the reality of the situation to the possibility of the situation.

Lesson 20

DON'T WORRY ABOUT THEM FOCUS ON YOU

Having a positive mindset focused on all the possibilities, rather than the barriers standing in your way, can not only increase motivation but also lead to an increase in confidence. That confidence in oneself is often called self-confidence for a reason. While the self refers to the object of confidence, it also refers to the source. Your confidence should stem from yourself: your preparation, your work, your focus, and your intentional thoughts. If you rely on your confidence to come from results, compliments, or other external sources, you are leaving your confidence up to chance. In 2013, I watched my dad successfully build a culture that cultivated a level of confidence in his team that allowed them to achieve things they had never accomplished before. Collectively, they were concerned with one thing—themselves—and they always came prepared to play the game.

That year, however, didn't come without challenges and emotional swings. The team faced both failure and criticism on its way to success, and away from the rink, my family experienced many personal highs and lows as well. Right before the season started, my grandfather, my dad's dad, passed away. Exactly five months to the day later, my mom's dad passed away. During the time in between their deaths, the Yale men's hockey team was in the middle of a season that found them nationally ranked. Right after my maternal grandfather passed away, Yale traveled to Atlantic City for the ECAC tournament. They were shut out completely as they lost the semifinal game and then the consolation game, 5–0 and 3–0 respectively.

Throughout the course of that season, our world at times felt completely out of control. We were processing losses and successes all at the same time, and I watched while my dad navigated attention as a coach on a scale I had never experienced before. Social media such as Twitter was more popular than ever and gave everyone a voice and a platform. There were a lot of comments, opinions, and voices, and as a college student, I was more aware than I had ever been before.

Following that 3–0 loss in the consolation game in Atlantic City, my dad made the unfavorable choice to skip the press conference, which resulted in a fine for the school. Scrolling through Twitter at the end of that weekend, I saw plenty of criticism being thrown at him for that decision, including one that said, "Yale should fire Keith Allain—team cannot handle any adversity #ecachockey."

Asshole, I thought. I knew better than to comment or engage, but I desperately wanted to defend my dad against this stranger on the internet. I clicked on his page, analyzed his photo, and scrolled through his Twitter feed as my mind formulated a response that I knew I would never type out. College and professional sports to some people are a hobby or interest that can spark stimulating conversations and debates at the local bar on a Friday night. In my life, it has always been personal. Countless times, I have had to bite my tongue, walk away, and scream all my thoughts and opinions silently as I listened to people, who usually didn't know who I was (but sometimes did and shared their thoughts anyway), ramble on with their uninformed opinions about people I loved and respected. As a young girl, I was hyperaware and concerned with what other people were saying, but I knew my dad wasn't. When I tried to bring a tweet or article to his attention, he would always respond with a shrug and say, "I don't read that stuff." It was just noise that he could hear but chose not to listen to.

You can't control other people, but more importantly, their opinions don't have any bearing on your performance unless you let them.

They are not the ones handling the puck on the ice or taking the shot. While many young athletes today have never known a world without social media that gives everyone a platform to speak, they aren't necessarily taught how to measure the value of an opinion or a voice. As a result, they are left on their own to navigate the treacherous course of comments and tweets, which have been shown to impact psychological well-being. In fact, a study examining time spent on social media prior to athletic competition found that it was correlated with sport anxiety and could compromise psychological readiness to perform.[27] Growing up watching my dad not just navigate but show no interest in the many voices and opinions that existed taught me that they didn't matter. He had no idea those tweets existed out in the world because he never took the time to check or read them. The only thing that mattered was his team.

Although that weekend in Atlantic City could have potentially ended my dad's season, twenty-four hours later, his team found out they were the last team to qualify for the

NCAA tournament, thanks to the ranking they had earned throughout the season. In the first game they played in the NCAA regional, they faced the number-one seed, the University of Minnesota. At the end of regulation, the game was tied at 2–2. I was watching from New Haven in a crowded Mory's on the Yale campus, and from across the room, I could hear the announcer, Sean Ritchlin, on TV as the overtime period began. "Well, Minnesota has the energy from the third period—you'd think that they would come out in the first few minutes and try to put this game away because they have the momentum and the energy." Before Ritchlin was done talking, the puck dropped, and Yale scored seven seconds into the overtime period, leaving not only Ritchlin but much of the college hockey world stunned.

For the next game in their regional, Yale faced North Dakota. Heading into the third period, they were down 1–0, but it wasn't an accurate reflection of the game. Yale outshot North Dakota in that game 39–25 and had a 25–16 advantage heading into that third period. Despite Yale's performance, I recall the announcers again heavily favoring their opponent. North Dakota's Hobey Baker finalists, their draft picks, and their history of success were all the announcers wanted to discuss. As I watched the game from our living room floor, making picture collages for my grandfather who had just passed away, I almost had to mute the TV. But actions, like my dad says, speak louder than words, and there was a lot of action happening on that ice.

Yale ended up defeating North Dakota 4–1 and punched a ticket to the Frozen Four. My phone rang as my mom called me from a sports bar in New Jersey where she was with my little brother for his own hockey games. I could tell that she was trying to hold back tears as we both watched the team celebrate on TV. My dad had just made the Frozen Four for the first time ever in Yale's history, but she knew she would have to miss it. She was flying home to Sweden for her father's funeral. We all wanted to attend the funeral with her but couldn't because of the travel, school, and the cost of flights.

On the internet, the public opinion that was expressed so strongly before was beginning to shift. One Twitter user even suggested that my dad should skip out on the press conference again, the same act that caused such criticism only seven days prior. "After last weekend, it worked this weekend," the tweet read. "If I was Keith Allain, I'd have avoided the West Regional press conference." While this time no one avoided the press conferences, they kept their focus and attention on themselves, making sure not to get distracted by anything or anyone else.

Players and coaches alike all echoed one another's responses as they discussed their team, their excitement, and their game to the media. It was clear that with their focus, the whole team was in sync both on and off the ice. This cohesion is one of the most important group variables when it comes to team success. In fact, due to cohesion's correlation with collective efficacy (or shared belief in a group's ability to succeed), a lack of cohesion has been highlighted as one of the factors that causes talented teams to fail to achieve their anticipated level of success.[28] One such example would be the 2004 USA Olympic men's basketball "dream team." They had more losses than any other USA men's basketball team at an Olympics and had to settle for bronze. As many media outlets pointed out, the team was made up of many skilled players who had never played together and had very little time to form that bond.

Cohesion is all about the group and the task at hand. While everyone else outside of the Yale hockey team tried to drown them with criticism after the ECAC tournament and overlooked them game after game throughout the NCAA tournament, they were the ones who continued to move forward.

More importantly, they kept their focus on themselves, despite what anyone else tried to get them to focus on, like their opponents.

In a story told by Steve Conn, Yale's communications director, he describes an interaction between my dad and some journalists at a press conference before the team left town and headed to the Frozen Four. The Ice Man was known for not wanting to discuss much with the media, but especially for not wanting to focus on anyone besides his own team. He frequently evaded questions and comments that referenced anyone who wasn't in his locker room. In the crowd that day before the Frozen Four, a brave reporter from Hartford spoke up and asked, "Can you appreciate the big picture for this state, with the two teams [in the Frozen Four]? It's been a very special time and it continues to be a special time for hockey in Connecticut. Is there any pause to appreciate that?" Steve Conn recalls my dad glancing at him, as he frequently did when he was asked a question he preferred not to answer. After his intentional eye contact with Conn, my dad leaned into the microphone and responded, "Not today," and left the room in an awkward silence. Further criticism followed that response, but my dad only had one concern, and it wasn't the critics.

When we began this section on emotion, I compared my dad's icy exterior and media presence to a more animated John Tortorella. While the two coaches may have some drastically different approaches to their job, this singular focus on their own team unites them. In 2019, Tortorella found himself back in Tampa Bay, where he won the Stanley Cup in 2004. This time, however, the Tampa Bay Lightning were his opponent, and he was the head coach for the Columbus Blue Jackets. While many wanted to welcome Tortorella back to Tampa and reminisce about the success they shared together many years before, he was not interested. "Don't even start talking to me about nostalgia and reminiscing," Tortorella said in an interview.[29] "I mean it. We are focused. I like this team that we have here in Columbus." And while Jon Cooper, the current Tampa Bay coach, was even willing to share some nice words about Tortorella as a coach and person to the media, Tortorella wasn't willing to do the same. "Yeah . . . I'm not interested in talking about the other team," Tortorella replied. In the end, Torts and his Blue Jackets swept the playoff series, eliminating the Lightning in four straight games. Their victory marked the first playoff series win in franchise history for Columbus and made Tampa the first team in history to finish first in the league and not win a single postseason game. Heading into that series, like Yale, there was a lot that Columbus could have worried about, but instead they focused on themselves.

After all the interviews and media, Yale finally got on the ice at the Frozen Four and secured yet another overtime win in the semifinal of the NCAA tournament. This time, my Twitter feed was flooded with a very different opinion. "Yale is going to win this whole damn thing," one tweet read. "Keith Allain is one of the best coaches in the game." But still, my dad didn't read any of it. His job wasn't complete, and he was focused on preparing his team. For that national championship final, the Bulldogs were set to face Quinnipiac, that other ECAC team that lived just down the road from Yale in

EVERYTHING I GOT | 156

Connecticut. At a press conference before that final game, a select few Yale players were sitting at the table addressing the media. Afterward, one journalist pointed out on Twitter that not a single Yale player even mentioned the word Quinnipiac in any of their responses. As Yale goalie Jeff Malcolm was quoted saying, "We understand what we are in our locker room, so we are just going to stick to our game plan."

Numerous psychological factors have been found to be debilitating to athlete confidence, which in turn impacts performance. Athletes are most likely to lose their confidence and ability to execute skills when they concentrate on factors outside of their control.

Ultimately, their control only lies within themselves—their preparation and their responses to the world around them.

Focusing on uncontrollable factors, such as your opponents and media, can greatly decrease that confidence and thus performance.[30] Another successful hockey player, Sidney Crosby, knows this. We mentioned earlier in this book how his routine on game days allows him to focus on his preparation and things within his control. One element of that routine is the path he takes entering the rink on game day and walking toward the locker room. Crosby does not go the most direct route, like many of his teammates. Instead, he takes a long detour, intentionally avoiding walking past the visiting team's locker room. While he hasn't specifically addressed any reason for the detour, we can imagine that a well-known player like himself may find a lot of distractions walking that traditional, more direct route. He most likely has friends on the other team, knows many people who want to chat, or perhaps knows there are even people who may want to heckle or distract him as he walks by. From a psychological standpoint, there is value in limiting any opportunity for his opponent, or anyone else, to occupy his mind or vision as he prepares himself to go out and play his game.

As a young woman in college during the time my dad and his team navigated the national stage, I took note. I watched every game, I listened to every interview, and I read every article. My dad had coached many successful teams prior to this point in my life, including winning a World Cup with Team USA, but this was the first time I was old enough to appreciate the accomplishment. More specifically, it was the first major athletic moment in my family that happened after my athletic career was over and I was beginning to consider sport psychology as a path for my future. Being able to see how the culture and the habits my dad had intentionally built throughout the years were coming to life in a very public way was both inspiring and intriguing. Not only did I see how little weight or importance the opinions of other people held, I also quickly learned how transient those opinions can be. Only mere weeks after people had urged Yale to fire my father, Twitter was flooded with comments praising both his actions and his coaching. But those comments, whether good or bad, didn't matter, and I learned that for any person trying to accomplish a goal, the most important place for you to direct your attention and focus is yourself and what you can control.

Lesson 21

THE PAST DOESN'T PREDICT THE FUTURE

As they prepared for that championship game, Yale wasn't preparing for an unknown opponent. In fact, they had already played Quinnipiac three times that year. They had lost all three games with a collective score of 13–3, as the media and everyone else liked to remind them. Looking at their past, anyone would have assumed Quinnipiac had a greater chance of winning the national championship that day than Yale: the number-one overall seed, who had handily beaten Yale three times already that season, versus the last team to qualify for the tournament. If Yale had focused on their opponent, they might have struggled to find their self-confidence. If Yale had focused on the media and what reporters were saying, they might have lost any self-confidence they had. However, no one's performance or journey is perfect. Luckily, they knew what many bettors that day I am sure failed to consider: the past doesn't predict the future.

On the day of the big game, after almost two scoreless periods, Yale hit the back of the net first with four seconds left in the second period. Heading into the third period of the game and final period of the season, they never looked back. With about seven minutes left in the national championship game, Yale scored its fourth goal, going up to 4–0.

I jumped about three feet out of my seat. As I landed on my feet, my siblings and I were both overwhelmed with joy and almost frozen with excitement. We didn't know what to do with ourselves. As celebrations continued occurring around me, I looked over in a haze at the team's bench, which was diagonally across the ice from me. Like a movie scene, I stood up on my chair, in an attempt to get a better view, and I saw my dad glance up in the direction of our section. I put my hands in the air, in celebration and almost disbelief. I pumped my arms as if to communicate, "Oh my god, we did it," across the ice. My dad, who was in the middle of coaching in a national championship game, lifted both his hands and motioned them downward in a slow and steady rhythm. He was telling me to settle down. The game wasn't over.

I sat back down and felt my phone buzz. There was a long, clearly international, number displayed on my screen. I looked at the time. It would have been about 3:00 a.m. where my mother was in Sweden. I answered and heard her frantic voice on the other end. "Oh my god . . ." was all I could hear through the poor connection and all the noise in the arena. "Are you watching?!" I yelled into my phone as she tried to explain that she was stressfully following a play-by-play update online. My grandmother's and uncle's voices behind her were cheering. It was a late night, after a long few days for them with my grandfather's funeral. However, it was joy and excitement I could hear in their voices for the first time all week. No one sounded sad or even tired. This game was giving us all reasons to smile and celebrate.

The final score of the game was 4–0, and Yale won their first ever national championship. Afterward, I had to listen to my dad tell our family and friends how he had to tell *me* to calm down in the middle of *his* game, but to be fair, as a coach, he was just telling us all—his players and me

included—what we needed to hear. Settle down; keep playing the game. In interviews after their victory, junior Kenny
Agostino once again verbalized the confidence that was
self-focused, not other-focused, but also their belief that
the past performances against Quinnipiac weren't going to
predict the outcome of this game. "We were confident in our
group," he said. "We knew we could win. We knew we could
do it. And we just took it by every game and again we worried about us, not any other team."

The obvious importance of not getting discouraged by
the previous losses that had no bearing on the outcome of
the current game is clear. The results of those games didn't
matter. But the past can have an impact, whether those
experiences were positive or negative. Could their past successes and victories have given Quinnipiac a false sense of
security heading into that championship game? Quite possibly. A study that examined gambling in college students
found that initial success led to more reckless decision-
making and, as a result, greater losses.[31] As Sam Weinman
puts it in his book *Win at Losing*, "Winning tends to seduce us
into thinking we've got it all figured out."[32] In other words, if
we rely too much on past successes to determine our future
success, we aren't dedicating the time necessary to prepare
and continue to improve.

That success cultivates a false sense of invincibility.

It would have been equally as beneficial for Quinnipiac as
it was for Yale to approach that game as an isolated event
rather than the fourth time they were playing a team they
had already beaten.

The winningest coach in Super Bowl history, Bill Belichick,

knows the importance of not getting too caught up with past success. With his six Super Bowl rings as the head coach of the New England Patriots and eight rings total, Belichick has plenty of success to reflect on. However, despite the amount of public attention he receives as a coach who will go down as one of the greatest ever, Belichick spends little time discussing his past accomplishments. For instance, at a Monday morning press conference after winning the 2016 Super Bowl, Belichick was quoted as saying, "As great as today is, in all honesty, we're five weeks behind thirty teams in the league in preparing for the 2017 season."

That quote epitomizes Belichick's philosophy, a philosophy that can be summarized in one key word: preparation. As seen by their composure under pressure, Belichick and his players find confidence in their preparation—not in the results or outcomes from previous games. Therefore, regardless of the circumstance, score, opponent, or play, they know what to do, what is expected of them, and they are fully ready to do their job. This was never more evident than at Super Bowl LI, when Belichick led the Patriots back from a 21–3 deficit at halftime to victory. He relied not on that first half to build their confidence or predict how the second half would go, but instead trusted their preparation and being present one play at a time.

For those who think he spends little time enjoying his success before moving on to prepare for the next challenge, he spends even less time focusing on potential future achievements. In a 2018 interview, Belichick was posed the question, "With all you have accomplished in your coaching career, what is left that you still want to accomplish?" Without hesitation, Belichick responded, "I'd like to go out and have a good practice today. That would be at the top of the list right now." Again, a loud and clear message to his team, and everyone listening, that the present moment is the only moment that matters.

Presence, like self-awareness, is fundamental to mindfulness. Mentally, our minds can be in many places. We can be contemplating and analyzing the past, wondering about the future, or present in the current moment. Physically, we can only be in the here and now. Mindfulness helps narrow our mental focus into the moment, which as a result helps improve our overall physical performance. Our mind and body need to align for us to be at our best, and the present is the only place they can both be.

Most of the emotional challenges that the athletes I work with face are retroactive, meaning that they stem from the past. We frequently get caught up in moments that have already passed and disengage ourselves from the present. These emotionally triggering moments can be mistakes made a few minutes ago, games played a few weeks ago, or even failures that happened years ago. These distractions not only take up valuable space in our minds, but also disrupt our ability to perform in the present.

However, just like our success yesterday doesn't guarantee us success today, our mistakes just a few minutes ago don't guarantee that we will mess up again right now.

We have to be willing to try again, despite our past failures, in order to have any chance of finding success.

Ted Lasso, the fictional but lovable football coach in the Emmy-winning series of the same name, may have said it best: "Do you know what the happiest animal in the world is?" Lasso asks his player. "It's a goldfish. You know why? It's got a ten-second memory. Be a goldfish." The focus is not on the past and not on the future. The focus is not on your opponent or the media. The focus is here and now, and on you and your game. Nothing else matters.

Part Three
GOALS

When it is all over, you will miss sitting in the locker room with your teammates talking about nothing, you will miss the nerves and excitement of game day, and you will miss all the moments that you were too busy trying to earn that you forgot to experience them.

The first time I was called "Coach" was strange for me. I imagine it is similar to the experience of being called "Mrs." for the first time after getting married. *Coach*, in my mind, was a term that was always associated with my dad and his job. *Coach* felt so official, so adult. I wasn't sure I was old enough or smart enough for it. I wasn't sure I had earned the title or the responsibility. I wasn't sure I really belonged there.

This experience, known as imposter syndrome, is one that many people can relate to. Oftentimes, people are found questioning themselves, their legitimacy, and whether they really deserve something or fit in. What I quickly realized about being a coach, however, was that the title wasn't something I deserved or earned because of my age or my education or even my experience. Those things may have given me the opportunity, but being called "Coach" was something I had to earn every day in my preparation and my interactions with my team.

Coaching, I realized, was far more than a simple title; it was a verb that required daily action.

More importantly, it was a new role and a new experience that I had never had before. Sure, I grew up with a coach and I studied coaches, but something changes when you are no longer wearing a jersey number but assigning them. As a result of this change, I had a different perspective that afforded me new realizations and, more importantly, new lessons.

The most alarming realization I had, which may have contributed to my feelings of imposter syndrome, was that the answers weren't always there. When you're a kid, there are a few people in your life who you believe have all the answers. For me, those people were my parents, my teachers, and my coaches. They knew everything I needed to know. Now I suddenly was the teacher and the coach, and the only thing I confidently knew was that I didn't have all the answers. While at first this was extremely intimidating, it also became freeing once I accepted that I didn't have to know everything. In fact, it became fundamental to my coaching and teaching philosophy. Once you let go of the idea that you should know everything or be able to do it all, the pressure of expectation transforms into an excitement of possibility. The first time I openly admitted, "I don't know," rather than trying to answer a question I had no answer to, I not only felt a weight lift off my shoulders but had doors open. I was able to discover solutions by acknowledging my limitations rather than restricting my own growth and learning.

Lesson 22

YOU DON'T HAVE TO BE THE BEST YOU JUST HAVE TO BE YOUR BEST

Early in my career, as I was discovering these new lessons, I was fortunate enough to work with many people who had faith in me even when I may not have been so self-assured. These people gave me opportunities to work with professional athletes, present to coaches who have had careers longer than I had been alive, and support teams at some of the most important sporting events of their lives. Being in all those new situations and sometimes questioning whether I belonged, I was often comparing myself to those around me by looking at their resumes and long lists of accomplishments.

Comparison, in general, is a dangerous game that we so often play in every facet of our lives: comparing your grades, your job, your salary, your success, and your life to those of the people around you. Those things aren't comparable because they are all parts of such different stories. Comparing yourself to the person next to you would be like trying to compare a touchdown in football to a basket in basketball or a goal in soccer. You score once in each sport, yet none of the values end up the same. The better approach is to compare yourself today to who you were yesterday. Did I learn from the experience and improve? Use that as your marker for success and growth.

One of the events I was fortunate enough to attend early on in my career was the NCAA women's rowing championship with the Yale women's crew team. I had spent the season working with the team implementing visualization scripts, doing mindfulness practice, and zeroing in on their self-talk and focus. Having no experience in crew as either a rower or a coach prior to that season, I relied a lot on the athletes' feedback to make sure the work I was doing was relevant to their experience on the water. I had worked with athletes competing in sports I had no experience in before, so I knew I could make an impact without being an expert at their craft. However, feeling knowledgeable about the skill set and the experience always helps me feel more confident in the process.

As we traveled to Indianapolis for the NCAA championship, my own self-doubt crept in as I felt out of my league preparing the team for the big stage. While I wasn't officially on the coaching staff, I was the youngest coach the team had with them. I was terrified of making a mistake and saying or doing something that would detrimentally impact their performance. As I had spent the first few days traveling with the team and taking in what was not just my first national championship meet but my first crew meet ever, I often wondered what I was doing there. I especially wondered how I could help a team with a history of success like Yale, which had fifteen top-ten finishes in the last eighteen years.

At the banquet for that NCAA championship, we had the honor to listen to the keynote speaker, Amanda Elmore, a member of the 2016 USA Olympic crew team. In her address, she shared some of her insight to the real thoughts, doubt, and nerves that even an Olympian can have. She candidly read us pages from the journal that she kept at those Olympic games. "So many amazing rowers have rowed this boat, and they picked me," she read. "I am the youngest, smallest, and slowest on the earth. I am terrified of messing up." *This is not the confidence you hope your athlete has heading into an Olympic race,* I thought to myself. "Every time I spiral into these thoughts," she continued, "I tell myself this: I am not the only one who can stroke and I might not be the best stroke, but I am stroking. No reason to wonder why I am here or if I should be. I just have to do my best. I know I'm not the best. I know I'm not perfect, and that's OK."

Sitting in the audience listening to Elmore read her journal, I was in awe of the parallels between her words and my feelings in that very moment. Just like Elmore knew she wasn't the best, I knew very well that I wasn't the best mental skills coach out there. I was a rookie who was still learning the ropes, not just of crew, but of the job in general. However, I just had to do my best in those moments and bring to the team everything I could. As Elmore continued reading, she began on her journal entry from the next day. "August 13, 2016: We did it . . ." Elmore and the rest of the USA women's eight team captured gold in Rio.

A few days after the banquet, the Bulldogs finished out the NCAA tournament as the eighth-fastest team in the country. Not only did they earn a top-ten finish, but most importantly, they improved on their own standing, finishing better than they started, as they had entered the weekend as the ninth-ranked team.

Focusing on simply being your best and believing in your ability to do so is confidence. Working with a lot of team-sport athletes, I have found that one of the barriers to overcoming a lack of confidence is the lack of clarity between what it means to be confident versus being cocky. While all athletes want to feel confident, they are hesitant to actively seek it out or display their confidence because they don't want it to be interpreted in a negative way. However, the difference is that cockiness is all about social comparisons—thinking you are better than other people.

Confidence has nothing to do with others and has everything to do with your own belief in yourself.

Consider a tryout situation, for instance. A cocky athlete would think or say, "I am the best person out here." In their mind, they might even go around the room and compare their ability to every other player there. "I am better than you," they think as they assess each individual, one by one. A confident athlete would simply think, "I believe in my own ability to make this team," and not feel the need to assess those around them at all. The point of confidence is not to place yourself above others but rather to instill a belief in yourself without even thinking about or focusing on your competition.

When I was working with a high school team on their overall group confidence one day, I began by asking them to go around and give the teammate beside them a compliment by identifying what made them a good player. They jumped right in, easily listing traits and skills of their teammates that they admired and how they contributed to the team. Once we had gone around the whole room, I instructed them to do the same thing again, but this time they had to identify their own strengths. The room suddenly went quiet. As we slowly went around the room, many of the responses began with statements such as "I guess . . . " and "I think . . . " rather than the powerful and definitive answers they had given for their teammates. We all tend to be more reserved and less comfortable talking about ourselves in a positive way than we do those around us. Part of this is because encouraging and supporting ourselves isn't an expectation, like supporting your teammates in a group setting is.

A few months after that NCAA championship, I received an email from Yale's head coach, Will Porter. "I have begun to think about next year," Porter began. "I really liked the way you were working with our team and feel like we were just scratching the surface." As he invited me to return to work with the team the following season, I realized other people were able to see my impact even when I couldn't. While I was busy doubting myself, they were busy noticing my ability. I felt uncomfortable acknowledging my own strengths, just like the girls in that exercise did, and relied on someone else to build my confidence for me.

Unfortunately, if we feel uncomfortable acknowledging our strengths and accomplishments, then the only times we are really talking or thinking about ourselves would be when we're discussing our mistakes, weaknesses, or mishaps. If we took a step back and analyzed ourselves in the same way we do other people, we would more often highlight positive things. This doesn't mean you have to high-five yourself every time you make a nice play or outwardly share all your successes, but you should take time to celebrate yourself and credit yourself for the hard work you do put in. Therefore, the first step for a lot of athletes to overcome the guilt and discomfort associated with building confidence and focusing on themselves is normalizing that. Simply asking yourself, "What did I do well today?" is an easy place to start. Remember, it isn't about what you did better than anyone else, but just about what you have done to help yourself become your best.

Lesson 23

EMBRACE FAILURE

In our process of becoming our best, some of the greatest educational experiences can be our own failures. However, it is an experience we exert a lot of effort and energy to avoid. We want success, and as a result, that is what we focus on in our goal-setting, in our visualization practices, and in our self-evaluations. What is it we want to win? How is it we will win? Did we win? The reality is, very few people experience "winning it all." Once you reach the playoffs, every team's season ends in a loss, except for one. Losing is one of the most common experiences in sport, but while we are in it, we often feel alone.

Part of this loneliness stems from the culture of success that we have cultivated as a society. Today more than ever, we idolize winners. We study them, we learn from them, and we worship them. In our media-driven world, those successful individuals are put on a pedestal along with their highlight-reel moments with their failures hidden in the shadows. As a result, it provides us with a skewed marker for how to measure our own progress and achievement as we try to live up to an incomplete picture.

In 2018, NFL quarterback Nick Foles was named the Super Bowl MVP as he led the Philadelphia Eagles to victory over the New England Patriots. When asked about his journey at the press conference following the big win, Foles reflected on the importance of failure as he said, "I think the big thing is don't be afraid to fail. In our society today—you know, Instagram, Twitter—it's a highlight reel. It's all the good things. And then when you look at it, you think when you have a rough day or your life's not as good as that, you're failing."[1] Foles, who was the backup until an injury sidelined the starting quarterback just a few weeks before the Super Bowl, was an unlikely hero for the Eagles that year. He had spent most of his career struggling to find a consistent starting position on an NFL team, and definitely did not seem to be a formidable opponent for Tom Brady, who was the quarterback for the Patriots. "Failure," Foles continued in the press conference, "is a part of life. That's a part of building character and growing. Like, without failure, who would you be? I wouldn't be up here if I hadn't fallen thousands of times, made mistakes . . . If something's going on in your life and you're struggling, embrace it, because you're growing."

A few months later, at training camp for the next NFL season, Kansas City Chiefs offensive coordinator Eric Bieniemy was faced with some tough questions about the progress, and more specifically recent failures, of another up-and-coming quarterback who threw seven interceptions as they prepared for the season. "It's been going good," Bieniemy said, despite the interceptions. "You know what, I will say this. He had a few hiccups today but that's part of the process. When you are young you need those hiccups because they become valuable lessons in life."[2] A year and a half later, that same quarterback, Patrick Mahomes, became the youngest quarterback in history to be named the Super Bowl MVP as he led Kansas City to victory.

I know Bieniemy is not the only coach or only person who has helped Mahomes reach his level of success, and there are a million other things that had to come together for him to achieve all that he has. However, I remember watching the interview and imagining how it must have felt for Mahomes to hear his coach support him in such a public way after struggling like he did with all that attention on him as he prepared for the season. Knowing that your coach still believes in you and isn't upset or concerned about the mistakes you made can relieve a lot of the pressure that causes athletes to overthink after a poor performance and, as a result, perform even worse in attempting to correct it.

At the first sign of trouble, many people panic, causing performance to decrease even more. This fear of failure exists in almost every facet of our society, and beyond the athletic field, schools are one of the biggest sources of this fear. Although failure is fundamental to the learning process and studies have shown that making more mistakes improves educational outcomes, it seems as though every effort has been made to eliminate the experience of failure from the educational system.[3] This is evident by the ever-increasing GPAs at academic institutions across the country. Ironically, as schools are allowing students to fail less, the value of their success is also decreasing. In a study that analyzed the consequences of the grade inflation that has occurred over the last thirty years, they explained that the grades that colleges and employers now see no longer can carry the same weight in determining whether a student has the necessary credentials.[4] As a result, grades that were meant to provide feedback are failing to offer any accurate insight. Furthermore, the study pointed out that as higher grades are awarded for average work, the work ethic of students is also deteriorating.

The story of the increasing average is really a story of decreasing failure. Failure has become unacceptable. Overall, the education system isn't designed for failure because its purpose isn't to limit students but to cultivate them. And I want to be clear: my point isn't necessarily that more students should be failing classes as a whole, but I think as educators and academic institutions, we need to allow for more failure in the process. Unlike Bieniemy, who was rewarding the effort Mahomes displayed and motivating him to push through the failure, these grades reward mediocrity as the final outcome and allow students to become complacent. Too often, teachers, parents, and coaches try to protect their kids from struggles that might offer more educational value than any of the content in our curriculums. This adversity can not only teach them resilience and persistence in the face of challenges but also encourage them to embrace more opportunities and appreciate their successes.

Unfortunately, the way our world is designed, we don't see value in the attempt or in failure because the results we prioritize can't be achieved simply through experiences or effort. Consider this: What is the first question we ask someone after a game, test, or other performance event? "Did you win?" "Did you ace it?" As an individual, what is it we tend to focus on when we set goals, both formally and informally? It's the end results: the scoreboard, the stats, the grade, the promotion, the title.

But the reality is, we can't all be winners. However, all winners know what it's like to lose; they just didn't let it stop them.

When it comes to adversity and opportunities for an athlete, March Madness is one of the biggest moments for any collegiate basketball player but also one of the most mentally challenging, with extreme amounts of pressure and attention. Popular news stories during the tournament always like to highlight any game that ended in a buzzer beater, a last-second shot to win the game—a pressure-filled moment that falls on the shoulders of a clutch player who is willing to embrace the challenge of the moment and rise to the occasion. Graham Betchart, a mental skills coach who has worked with numerous NBA athletes, explains the mindset of those clutch players who are able to make that last shot in the toughest of circumstances.[5] "Failure," he explains from their perspective, "is not missing the shot; it's, 'I didn't take it.' It's a complete shift, where everyone else is obsessed with winning and losing, which is paralyzing." This mindset that focuses on taking the shot, not on making the shot, not only takes pressure off of the result but embraces the opportunity in the moment. It is the mere effort or attempt at the goal that makes one successful, not the outcome. This is similar to when I encouraged my figure skater in her goal-setting process to just jump and make the commitment to go for it, regardless of the result.

Goal-setting has always been a central feature of sport psychology, and I believe this process of accepting loss and embracing our failures begins with our goals. Research has shown that setting goals can help you focus your attention and sustain your motivation—two critical components of success.[6] However, many people have goals and still struggle with those things. Many people set goals and then never reach them. Many people set goals and then think they can check the mental portion of their training off the list. It isn't that simple.

The biggest misconception that I see the first time I set goals with athletes is the expectation that arises that by setting the goal they will achieve it. Their disappointment and embarrassment when we meet a week later and they confess to me they didn't achieve their weekly goal is evident. They failed. Their reaction when I don't match their emotion is confusion. How am I not upset with them? If they tried, if there is obvious effort, just no results, how can I be upset? Goal-setting isn't about the result, but about the process that it ignites.

A goal, by definition, is something you strive for. It is far more than a to-do list. If my athletes set three goals and achieve all three easily within a week, then I know they aren't pushing themselves enough. That list isn't a goal sheet, but rather a list of things they can already do.

Failure is an integral, but often overlooked, part of the goal-setting process.

In fact, the dictionary definition of *strive* includes the word *struggle*. If my athletes set a goal and don't reach it right away, then I know they are truly striving for something. If they are accomplishing their goals with relative ease, then we aren't doing enough to move ourselves forward. US national champion figure skater Bradie Tennell described this process in a clever way when asked about her consistency and process as she prepares her new skating programs. "I want to grow into my programs like a little kid trying to buy shoes," she explains. "I don't want it to be a perfect fit right away because that limits the amount of progress I can make."[7]

If we can conceptualize failure as an integral part of our goal-setting process and normalize the experience for ourselves by preparing for setbacks, then the losses will simply be a step along the way rather than a roadblock. Furthermore, by accepting failure, like we do our emotions, we regain control and are able to use it to motivate us to continue to grow rather than paralyze us in disappointment. This motivation from failure was highlighted by major league baseball player and two-time world series champion Johnny Damon in his letter to his younger self posted on the Players' Tribune website. As Damon says, "That frustration and sense of failure you feel? It's important. In a weird way, it's actually good for you. This is a majority failure sport. Nobody succeeds at the plate more than they fail . . . so even when you lose, if you keep the right mindset, you'll never be defeated. You're always going to remember the feeling of losing during those early years, and it's going to make your desire to succeed that much stronger."[8]

Every time we fall, we learn far more about ourselves, our ability, and our toughness than we do when we achieve things. While the process required to win is difficult, the act of winning itself is the easiest thing in the world. Losing is hard. Losing isn't fun. Losing is where we learn and become better. Take US swimmer Missy Franklin, for instance. In 2016, Franklin arrived in Rio at the Olympic Games as a reigning Olympic champion. She had won five medals, four of which were gold, as a seventeen-year-old four years earlier in London, and at the time of the 2016 games, she was the world-record holder in the two-hundred-meter backstroke. However, despite all the expectations, in Rio, she only won one gold medal, and that was for the team relay, which she only participated in during the preliminary heat. She didn't even make the finals in her two best events: the two-hundred-meter freestyle and two-hundred-meter backstroke. When asked about what she learned through her week of adversity in Rio, numerous media outlets reported that she said, "Ask me again in a few weeks. Right now, it sucks." Years later in a podcast interview, Franklin said the following: "Rio was without a doubt one of my biggest failures within my career, but as a person it was one of my greatest successes. Because I am so proud of how I handled myself and of how I got through that and how I still showed up for my teammates even when I was having the worst eight days of my life. And so, I think that's kind of the beautiful thing about failures: they may be failures in one sense of the word, but you do have that power to potentially turn it in to one of your greatest successes."[9]

If you never lose, you will never reach your full potential because there are so many lessons you have not had the opportunity to learn with only knowing what it is like to succeed. When you set goals, a bad goal only gives you one type of experience: success. A good goal requires you to fall a few times before you accomplish it. That failure is simply the early process of success.

Lesson 24

SHOOT FOR THE MOON BUT DON'T LOSE YOUR HEAD IN THE CLOUDS

Although essential to that process, failure can be difficult for many people to manage. It seems counterproductive for success. However, we now know it is not counterproductive but rather helping you grow and improve to become more successful. One thing that can help prevent us from getting too overwhelmed by the delay sometimes caused by failures is shifting our vision away from the end goal and paying attention to the small goals we can achieve in the moment. If we set goals that require us to strive but break them down into smaller steps to guide the way, then we can find success in every day and stay present in each moment. Responding to adversity can even be a goal we set so then that failure isn't a letdown but suddenly an opportunity. As a result, those smaller victories allow us to enjoy the process and fuel our motivation while still pushing us to reach for tomorrow.

This process of shifting our focus and finding success in the moment challenges the way we traditionally look at and define success. At the end of my first session with any athlete, I typically have them complete the following sentence: "Success is . . . " The most common answers are ones that are directly associated with achieving a goal of some sort: being a Division I athlete, winning a game, or winning the championship. When we define our success, it is almost always defined by accomplishing a long-term goal. However, a lot is going to happen between now and achieving those goals, and sometimes those lofty aspirations can cause us to get lost along the way and lose some of our motivation.

One athlete I had defined success with an extremely long-term goal of "being happy when you are sixty-five and retired." I laughed as he completed the sentence and then responded, "So we have a long way to go before we can experience any success, apparently." He shrugged shyly and tried to defend himself, but he suddenly realized the connection I was about to make. We had just spent the last hour discussing his mindset when he played, and his concern with not being on the score sheet. He was worried about his stats in the game because he was worried about the draft at the end of the season, where he would play next year, and how that would impact his life beyond that. His focus was constantly on the future and all these goals he wanted to achieve, and never in the present moment. This not only impacted his ability to execute anything on the ice effectively but also inhibited him from experiencing true joy or satisfaction with anything he was doing. He was never going to see himself as successful because there was always something else he needed to obtain down the road. As a result, he was never fully present in the moment to help himself actually achieve that success.

Former NHL player and Hockey Hall of Fame member Adam Oates has also noticed this challenge of being present in many hockey players. He has spent most of his time since his retirement coaching. After a short stint coaching NHL teams, Oates found a role as a private coach for many of the elite players currently in the NHL, working on their skills and hockey IQ. Reflecting on his work with some of the best hockey players in the world, Oates has said the most common mistake he has to address comes down to one question: "When you go out for forty-five seconds," Oates asks, "are you paying attention all forty-five seconds?"[10] He knows it sounds odd at first, but the fact of the matter is that whether it is outcomes, fatigue, or past mistakes, we all have a tendency for our mind to drift away from the actual task at hand.

Elite athletes and coaches are highly driven and goal oriented. This can be great for motivation, but it can also test our ability to stay focused on the task at hand and be detrimental to our overall well-being. Many athletes, like the one I mentioned before, are constantly striving for the next thing. They want to score more goals so they can make the best team. Once they make the team, they want to get recruited to a good school. If they make it to that school, then they feel the need to perform at a certain level to impress the scouts.

It is as if they are constantly running on a treadmill that never allows them to reach a new destination, which is both mentally and physically exhausting.

Even coaches can make the same mistake. Years ago, I was able to sit down and have a conversation with Wayne Wilson, the head coach for Rochester Institute of Technology's men's hockey team, who discussed this challenge as he said, "I think so many coaches don't get to enjoy the good years. The bad years stick with them forever; they don't seem to ever get over a bad year. But a good year you seem to get over real quick, and you move on to the next game." The next game, the next goal, the next job is always there waiting to make our success feel short lived.

When we achieve one thing we have been working toward, instead of celebrating that success, we just shift the bar of success even higher. While I always encourage my athletes to aim high and shoot for the moon, I want to make sure their minds don't get lost in the clouds on the way there. Even while we are striving for long-term goals, we want to stay grounded in the present moment and not overlook the things we should be doing and the success that can exist in the here and now. Otherwise, they get lost in a no-man's land where they are dreaming about the future but unable to execute in or appreciate the present.

If you are an athlete who has those lofty long-term goals, we do not want to eliminate the aspirations that fuel you. However, we do want to make sure you don't get burnt out chasing after success that is continuously out of your reach. Finding success in each and every day doesn't diminish the desire to strive for more. In fact, research has shown that celebrating small successes increases motivation over longer periods of time.[11] A simple approach to this is to break up your big goals into smaller, more manageable pieces—process goals, as most people refer to them as. Not only do these process goals provide you with guidance as you work toward your ultimate end goal, but they also give you something to celebrate along the way.

One way to create those process goals is to identify the actionable steps that you need to take to achieve your goal. If you want to play at a good Division I school, you might spend the next few months focusing on a goal of improving a certain skill set or strengthening your body. For the athlete I mentioned before who was worried about his stats, we needed even smaller process goals focused on his actions in the moment during the game. As we discussed it, I asked him to write down everything he needed to do in the game in order to score a goal and get on the stat sheet. He created a list of six things, which included winning battles, making tape-to-tape passes, keeping his head up, driving to the net, creating space, and communicating. Then I had him check off the things on the list that he was doing well and circle the ones he wasn't. He checked off four out of the six things in his list.

When I first saw his response, I congratulated him and celebrated the things he was doing well. Based on his initial evaluation of his performance, I would have never imagined he would check off four out of six things. He was doing more than half of them and doing them well. This moment allowed him to see how his emotions and frustration were blocking his ability to see his strengths and what he had been able to accomplish. Things were not as bad as they seemed, and needing to improve only on two specific areas felt very manageable. That realization alone was more motivating than simply focusing on the score sheet.

Then, in order to help him improve, we took those two items that he circled and used them as the foundation for his process goals for his upcoming games. Whether he scored or not, we could evaluate his success the following week based on what was happening in the moment of the game and not on the outcome. While these were still stretch goals that required him to improve, and maybe fail in the process, they were much more attainable in the moment and motivating. Suddenly he was thinking about what he needed to do right now, and not where he wanted to be some day in the future.

If you are a coach who struggles with finding or enjoying your success in the moment, as Wilson had mentioned, then you may need to reevaluate your definition of success and make sure it isn't constantly stuck in the future out of reach, like my athlete's interpretation of success was. In that same conversation, Coach Wilson gave me insight to a new concept of a successful season. He told me a story about their first year as a Division I program at RIT during the 2005–2006 season. As a new Division I team, they didn't officially belong to a league, and therefore most of their games were on the road as they traveled to other schools trying to build a Division I schedule. He couldn't remember the exact number of wins they had that first year when we spoke, which told me it didn't really matter in the grand scheme of things, but I looked up their record for that season after our conversation out of curiosity. They went 6–22–2. They only won 20 percent of their games. Yet, this is how he described that year: "It was one of the teams I was more proud of. They competed hard all the time, and they came to the rink every day. . . . That was a year that I was very happy about, and if I looked at the record you go, 'How could you be happy about that? And it had to be a long year.' But I didn't think it was at all, it was kind of fun to come to the rink."

At the time, I couldn't imagine it being fun to come to the rink when you lose 80 percent of your games. I had assumed that when he referenced a bad year earlier in our conversation, that a 6–22–2 record would fall into that category— something that may even haunt him to this day, keep him up at night. But instead, he spoke of that experience almost with a sense of nostalgia and longing.

Winning, I realized, doesn't define the good and bad, or success and failure.

More importantly, if we are constantly searching for the next win, we won't appreciate the ones we get. The team was striving for plenty of new goals in its transition to a Division I program, but it was the effort and the culture of that team in its day-to-day actions that made the year a success.

When it comes to creating that culture of enjoyment and effort, appreciating small goals or victories in your team is crucial. Jim Calhoun, former UConn men's basketball coach and three-time national champion, was known to do this. He would celebrate daily wins, no matter how big or small they were. Anything from a great play in practice, a player passing an exam, or a weight room personal best were all honored, and those moments contributed to the motivating culture of the team.[12]

When we set our goals, we want to aim high and shoot for the moon. However, it is important to not get too far ahead of ourselves in that process and be unable to live in the moment. As we know, when all is said and done, it is that process that gives us the most pride, and we don't want our misplaced minds to cause us to lose out on it.

Lesson 25

OUR GREATEST REWARD
IS OUR EXPERIENCE

While we are searching for success to motivate us in our day-to-day lives, one of the most common and powerful things to celebrate is the moment itself—not just the hard work that you are proud of, but the experiences you get being an athlete. Rather than constantly chasing after the next goal, reminding yourself to stay present in the here and now allows you to appreciate where you are, how far you have come, and the moments you are fortunate enough to have.

Many successful athletes have understood the value of not getting too caught up in the race for results and embracing the opportunities when you get them. Tennis player Naomi Osaka, for instance, could have been overcome with stress and anxiety when she got the opportunity to play against Serena Williams in the first round of the Miami Open in 2018. When asked about her nerves before playing the big star, Osaka responded, "My whole life, I've always wanted to play her. So, I had nothing to be nervous about."[13] Echoing her same mentality was hockey player Jack Hughes in 2019, when he was the youngest member of the USA hockey team at the World Junior tournament. After he was projected as the number one overall draft pick for that upcoming year, all eyes were on Hughes and what he would accomplish on the big stage. When asked about the pressure and expectations, he responded, "There's no nerves. That's what you want as a kid. For me it is exciting, and I am sure most of the guys will say that. It should be a big stage and should be a lot of fun."[14] Both Osaka and Hughes could have been overwhelmed with what they were expected to accomplish or achieve in those moments, but instead, they realized the moment itself was something to celebrate and enjoy, not wish away while rushing toward a result.

I often work with athletes as they struggle with anxiety before big events. One time, as I was helping an athlete prepare for the international stage and she was discussing her fears, I asked her a question that I have asked many athletes before: "What would be the absolute worst-case scenario for you?" She thought about it and responded, "Putting all this energy into something and not getting anything out of it." I considered that for a moment and then asked, "What would be the best-case scenario?" Once again, she took some time to think about it and responded, "I would succeed and be considered a top athlete. I would get to travel and compete all over the world. I would be improving every day and having so much fun."

Fear and anxiety typically stem from the idea or possibility of the worst-case scenario, especially in the case of performance. For this athlete, when she discussed the fear of "not getting anything out of it," the "it" was the hard work, the hours of practice, and the sacrifices she had made for her sport—having it all be for nothing. Initially, when she explained the dilemma of sacrificing so much for nothing in return, I assumed she meant she wouldn't get a medal or win. What interested me the most about our conversation, however, was that her best-case scenario highlighted many things that she would gain regardless of the outcome of her performance.

The experience, or her journey, was her best-case scenario. When she took the time to think about it, the opportunity to travel, getting the chance to compete, and having fun while continuing to improve was the best outcome she could think of. The result, the trophy or medal or whatever the reward she would receive for winning, was simply considered icing on the cake.

But the truth is, many of us are already eating the cake but forgetting to savor every bite.

She was already a top athlete who was traveling all over the world to compete and having fun. None of that was going to change or be taken away from her, regardless of the outcome of the competition she was worried about. If she took the time to realize what she already had, she would know that she had already gained so much out of "it." Her responses from that conversation reflect many of the answers I often get from my athletes. Their worst-case scenarios are not losing or failing, but not being able to play anymore, not being able to get that experience and having the moment, not the medal, taken from them.

You hear it often if you speak to people who have reached the pinnacle of their sport: the Olympics, the Stanley Cup, the World Cup. When asked about their experiences at those events, their biggest regrets are often that they almost missed it. Everything was so crazy and it went by so fast. Suddenly it was over and all they thought about was winning, and whether they achieved that or not, they realized they missed so much else.

When I was at the 2018 Olympics in PyeongChang, I was fortunate enough to chat with Arielle Gold, bronze medal snowboarder. She was the youngest member of the half-pipe team four years earlier in 2014 but had suffered an injury before she was able to contend for a spot on the podium. This time, however, she didn't miss her chance to compete or her chance to enjoy the Olympics as both an athlete and a fan. I ran into her outside of the hockey rink in Gangneung, a few hours from the nearest mountain. Her Olympics were "over," she explained, as she walked around with her bronze medal hanging proudly around her neck. Her events were all done, and she had no more competing left to do. However, she wanted to stay and meet people and watch other events because at her last Olympics she didn't get to experience any of that. She flew in and flew out, not seeing much else besides the mountain. While so much of an athlete's time at the Olympics is typically spent "behind the scenes" in preparation, she didn't want to rush home like many Olympians do after their events are complete. She was wise enough to appreciate the moments after her competition and soak up every bit of the experience. Unfortunately, most of us don't get two chances to go to the Olympics to teach us that lesson.

Sometimes even the most challenging moments that we try to wish away or overlook can be the most valuable ones. Once, I was working with an athlete who was a hockey player. He was a defender, but his coach had switched him to forward. This change frustrated him and tested his confidence because he wasn't able to showcase his abilities and his strengths in the new position as well as he would have been able to do as a defender. More specifically, this occurred during a time when he was trying to get recruited to play at the next level, and the scouts would not be able to see him at his best if he were out of his element on the ice. The decision was out of his control, and the outcome seemed hopeless at times. In all our sessions, it was clear that he wanted to just get through this difficult time period so he could move on and move forward past this adversity toward better things.

Fast-forward two and half months later, and together we were reflecting on all the changes he had endured in the season so far. He was back in his usual position, but on a different team. In the previous weeks, he had moved to a different state, transitioned to online learning, started living alone for the first time, and adjusted to new teammates and coaches. In our conversation, I asked him to list two to three things that he had improved on since the season started in October, and the first thing he said was, "I have become more offensive in my game." This caught my attention, and I asked him if he thought that came as a result of the experience he had at forward earlier in the season. He paused to think for a moment and agreed, although a bit reluctantly. As he explained, playing forward showed him a new perspective on the ice, and it gave him a different experience of the game. Once he was finally back in his position, he was able to use that to get involved with the offense more effectively as a defender. Although he wouldn't want to have to switch positions again, he was able to realize that he learned a lot from the experience he had as a forward.

Difficult experiences can teach us many lessons, but it may require a greater sense of self-awareness and discipline to appreciate those moments and grasp them when they come. It is easy to learn a lesson when it is presented to you in class, given to you in a review packet, and then reinforced in a test or a quiz. It is easy to spot the lessons that a coach or a teacher is explicitly delivering to you and instructing you to implement. It is much more challenging to find the lessons hidden in your world like a never-ending Easter egg hunt, requiring you to stretch your arms to reach the one on the highest branch of the tree, or wade through the bushes and weeds where some may be hidden from plain sight. You have to remain vigilant, and you have to keep your eyes open.

The lesson isn't always highlighted in bold, but the key is to never stop looking for them and never stop learning from every moment we are fortunate enough to have.

It is very common for us to get so mesmerized by our future goals or sidetracked by failure, or even just the possibility of it, that we overlook the present and the value and greatness that can exist in the things we already have and the moments we get to experience. Katie Ledecky emphasized the importance of these moments when she was asked by parents for some advice during a media event one day. Ledecky is a US Olympic swimmer who has won seven Olympic gold medals and fifteen World Championships, yet she was a bit baffled when a parent asked her how they could help their young daughter become the "next Katie Ledecky." Reflecting on her swimming career, she couldn't recall being in such a hurry to become what she is today or achieve the amazing accomplishments she has. "I feel lucky that I could enjoy swimming," she said. "It's not about immediate results. . . . Embrace the chase of those ahead of you. The times will come and you will have fun getting there."[15]

Embrace the chase of those ahead of you in the pool. Embrace the chase of the things ahead of you in your goals. While embracing the chase acknowledges the things that are in front of you, it also encourages you to embrace the process and the moment you are in, to enjoy and appreciate the moments of struggle, hard work, and fun. Too often, I have spoken with athletes who have finished their careers and told me they wish they had taken the time to appreciate those moments more. When it is all over, you will miss sitting in the locker room with your teammates talking about nothing, you will miss the nerves and excitement of game day, and you will miss all the moments that you were so busy trying to earn that you forgot to experience them.

Lesson 26

DON'T BE AFRAID TO DO THINGS DIFFERENTLY IF YOU WANT DIFFERENT RESULTS

As we work toward our goals and try to earn each moment, sometimes we hit a wall. That wall may be physical or mental, but either way, we find ourselves stuck and unable to move beyond our current standing. In times like these, frustration can grow when we keep doing the "right things" but aren't seeing any of the right outcomes. However, it is important to note that there is no universal right or wrong approach to success, and so sometimes we may need to try something different than what we have been doing in order to break down that wall. In goal-setting specifically, while some people have tried to claim that there is a "right way" to set goals, I have found success using many different approaches based on the needs of my athletes.

Goal-setting has become one of the pillars of sport psychology that everyone can lean on. With multiple publications backing its claims, setting goals is considered to be as fundamental to success in all domains as brushing your teeth is to your oral and physical hygiene.[16] You brush your teeth in the morning to start off the day. You set your goals before you start to give yourself direction. You brush your teeth at the end of the day to clean off any plaque or germs that have accumulated. You reassess your goals at the end of a game, season, or set time frame and reset to move forward.

An abundance of the research out there is focused on a specific type of goals: SMART goals. While there are a few different versions of this acronym that defines the goal-setting process, the most common stands for Specific, Measurable, Attainable, Relevant, Time-Bound.[17] The purpose of SMART goals is to formalize a process that many people already do casually. Having goals is human nature. Setting them in a format that optimizes your chances of achieving them is data-driven science. When I began coaching, I eagerly implemented these types of goals with the athletes that I worked with as I had learned to do from my research and studies examining high achievers.

Structurally, the process makes sense. However, in this puzzling world of sports and performance, I quickly learned that nothing is a guaranteed success. Convincing my athletes to write their goals down, clearly define them based on these parameters, and assess their progress periodically doesn't give me the gold star of mental skills coaching. It may be SMART, but the more experience I gained trying to help different athletes, the more I started to think it may not always be wise to just follow the predetermined guidelines. Therefore, I began to evaluate my approach and spent a lot of time trying to identify why these goals weren't as effective as I was told they would be when I was working with my athletes at the beginning of my career.

What I realized was that most of the athletes I work with have gotten to a high level in their respective disciplines because they are already measuring and assessing their performance. Not only are many of them doing it on their own, but their coaches and others around them continued to emphasize their daily, weekly, and season-long goals without my help or encouragement. As I reflected on our process together, I began to understand that they didn't need me to reinforce that again. They didn't need me to remind them of their timeline and the measurable aspects of their performance such as the scoreboard, the standings, their skill development, or the championship at the end of the season. So, rather than focus on the SMART process other people had told me would work, I needed to try to help my athletes identify an approach that would work for them and their unique needs and situations. There was no universal definition of what made a good goal, and in the ever-changing context of sports, and life, sticking to a rigid structure can limit our growth more than it promotes it.

Therefore, I decided to try something different in order to get different results than what I was seeing. I started paying more attention to when my athletes became motivated and why. I wouldn't say they were all driven by instant gratification, but they definitely liked seeing results. Long-term goals felt overwhelming and were so far off in the distance; short-term goals were a bit more effective, focusing on things they could do now—like those process goals I already mentioned. However, more than just a result or successfully executed skill, they were also motivated by feelings, frequently reflecting on how certain games or performances felt, something that seemed unmeasurable.

As a result, I decided to shift their goals and their focus to the experience, not the product.

I wanted to set goals that focused on how things made them feel in the moment. I wanted them to be proud. I wanted them to feel good about themselves. I wanted them to be happy.

While goal-setting primes you to focus on the destination, it is the process that makes all the difference—the process of training and preparing, but also the process of goal setting. The experience of setting goals, striving for them, failing, reflecting, and adjusting is far more impactful than the moment of accomplishment at the end. In this goal-setting process, I think the most important and overlooked step is self-reflection. In order to break down the wall I was experiencing with many of my athletes in terms of their progress and mindset, I had to reflect on our goal-setting process and let go of the methods that I had seen other people use and focus on what my athletes needed in that moment. Whether it be suffering from mental or physical exhaustion, burnout, or just excessive pressure, they needed goals that shifted their attention away from the performance result, or even their performance at all, and back to their reason for playing. These are two of my favorite goals I started setting for the athletes I worked with:

- Laugh every day at the rink/field/gym
- Make yourself proud every day

First, let me acknowledge that setting the goals for the athletes myself is a sport psychology faux pas from the very start. For goals to be as motivating as possible, many believe that they should come from the athlete. Telling them what to do isn't as powerful as them determining it themselves. But there are no absolutes in life, and there are certainly no absolutes in sports. Sometimes you have to do things differently if you want different results. So I began assigning some goals for them, focused on elements of their athletic experience that I knew they had been overlooking and wouldn't have been able to focus on themselves. As you try to help people shift their mindset, I realized, sometimes you need to scaffold the process for them and lead the way before they can do it autonomously.

Those two goals I shared are completely unrelated to a skill set, a performance outcome, or even a specific sport. While you could measure or count the laughs you have every day, making yourself proud is a bit more difficult to quantify. Yet, you can still assess it. I know because I've tested it. My athletes can tell me with 100 percent accuracy, if they choose to be honest, if they are proud of themselves or not, and they can tell me why. It would have no reliability in research because each person's assessment of their own pride will vary. Some may be proud of simply showing up to practice, while others wouldn't be proud unless they pushed themselves at practice.

However, our goals aren't about comparing ourselves to each other; they are our own unique journey.

More importantly, that individual journey will vary day to day. There are some days when even the toughest competitors don't feel like going to the gym or to practice, but getting up and going is something to be proud about. As a result, these goals allowed for my athletes to check in with themselves daily, identify where they were, and find something good in each day. These may have been more ambiguous goals than the traditional goals athletes set, but it didn't make them any less impactful. In my opinion, they were more heartfelt and inspiring. There was more emotion and motivation in these goals than any SMART goal I had set with an athlete. We can't get stuck thinking that goals are just about performance outcomes, because we know the results aren't always why we do these things and work so hard, and it isn't what we are proud of at the end of the road. It is our process.

We do things because they are fun. We do things because we love them. We do things because we gain a lot from those experiences. If we shift our focus during our goal-setting to the things we gain, rather than the things we might lose— like a game or a medal—then our goals can reset our mindset away from the pressure and anxiety that come along with elite performance. This shift can help us battle those nerves that we will feel. It can remind us to have fun in the midst of all the other stuff that doesn't actually matter: the wins, the losses, the contracts, the medals, the sponsorships . . . whatever it may be.

Now, changing the way we do things can be scary, especially if we have been doing things a certain way for a long time. The hardest athlete to convince they need to do something differently is the one who has had some success with what they are currently doing. "But that's what got me here," they say. "No, we shouldn't change that. It's been working," pointing to themselves as clear evidence. And it is true: it worked. It worked so well it got them on the varsity team, to a Division I school, to a national tournament, or even earned them a professional contract. That is great. It is particularly great if that is all they wanted to accomplish.

However, if you want to do more, if there are still goals left out there you want to achieve and steps forward you have not been able to take, that may require something different.

Because you haven't done those things yet, so what you are doing hasn't gotten you *there*.

Maybe your rigorous training pushed you to the level you are at, but an effective recovery routine is what will provide you with more benefits of your training and elevate you to the next level. Maybe your perfectionism has disciplined you to become the elite athlete that you are, but accepting flaws and mistakes will help you approach your job with more consistency now that the pressure, nerves, and competition are greater than ever before. Changing the way I approach goal-setting with the athletes I work with may seem like a small detail, but it was something I was nervous about doing. It took me outside of a safe and secure comfort zone, where I had research and experts backing up my approach. However, if I just kept doing things that way because it was what I, and others, had always done, I would have limited the impact I could have on my athletes. Each person and each situation is different. As you move forward, you may need to change your routines and things you do to adapt to the new context. Being willing to adjust and change to achieve new things and reach new heights is critical for your continued growth. Change is scary but can also be necessary.

Lesson 27

LAUGH EVERY DAY

Out of all the techniques I have tested and tried with athletes, a playful mindset is the one that I have seen open the most doors to success, by any definition. However, sometimes when I suggest the above goal about laughing, that is what I get in response: laughter. Athletes, parents, and even coaches think it's cute, but they don't think it is a goal for an elite, competitive athlete. Trust me, I am as competitive as the next person. I don't condone participation trophies. When you lose, you lose. You have to be OK with losing to be grateful for the win. But you also need to laugh to perform, and this is something that becomes prioritized less and less as the pressure and stakes begin to rise.

What people often overlook as they dismiss the importance of joy in performance is the impact laughter has on your body physically. When you are laughing, you are physically loose, which allows your body to execute any necessary motor tasks with fluidity and precision. Ever try shooting a basket, kicking a ball, or swinging a bat when your body was really tense? It is anything but smooth. What happens when you make a mistake? Well, if you can't shake it off and laugh at yourself, then your next attempt will be stiff and most likely worse than the first attempt.

Beyond the execution of a task, laughter can improve your mood and alleviate the mental side effects of stress.[18] This all happens because of the hormones and chemicals that are released in your body when you laugh. Laughter decreases stress hormones, activates the reward system in your brain, and releases serotonin, a natural antidepressant. When your head is filled with negative thoughts, laughter can help you erase them and not just find the good but force yourself to focus on it. Despite the value in a good laugh and the simplicity of a goal requiring you to laugh every day, accomplishing that goal in a high-performance environment will require you to strive for it and fail a little along the way. It isn't always easy to find the humor and joy when things are tense and stressful. More specifically, it is hard to find the perfect balance of taking yourself seriously enough to reach your full potential and laughing at yourself in the process.

A few years ago, I attended the Association for Applied Sport Psychology conference in Toronto, where one of the speakers was mental performance coach and author Jean-François Ménard. Ménard, who has worked with many Canadian Olympians, began his career helping Cirque du Soleil performers deal with the pressure to perform. I recall Ménard revealing during his presentation in Toronto that day that, across all the clients he has had, the most emotionally intelligent performers were the clowns at the Cirque du Soleil. The intrapersonal and interpersonal intelligence required to manipulate their own behavior and emotional expressions to make people laugh was one that still impressed him years later after having worked with numerous gold medalists and world champions. More specifically, it often required vulnerability from the clowns to make themselves the butt of the joke.

This humility is a trait that many high achievers share.

Being unafraid to laugh at ourselves, whether it be a mistake, an embarrassing moment, or an intentional act to alleviate the tension in those around us, is maybe the most underrated key to success.

In that letter I mentioned written by Johnny Damon to his younger self where he discussed the importance of failure, he exemplified this, as he also emphasized the value of laughter. "You need to have fun in order for the wins to come," he explains. "Creating that association between winning and fun in Boston is going to change your life. . . . For starters, you'll be the king of pranks. If you ever have a chance to tie someone's shoelaces together, do it. If you feel like walking around the clubhouse naked, do that too. I mean, your teammates will definitely be a little caught off guard, but there's something about unexpectedly seeing a teammate naked before a game that gets your mind right for some reason. Not sure what it is, guess it's just science. And the looser you and your teammates are, the better you'll play. . . . While they're thinking about how ridiculous you are, they won't be worrying about the pitcher they'll be facing that day or how important it is to win that game."

Damon isn't the only prankster in professional sports. Many professional sports teams and organizations have long-standing traditions when it comes to pranks and jokes inside the locker room and around the game. Stories of stolen clothes, fake snakes, prank calls, and more are all a part of the culture for these serious professional athletes. In the NHL, for instance, any rookie who gets the honor to lead their team out of the tunnel for warmups on their NHL debut is at risk for an awkward lap or two around the ice all alone while their teammates watch from the tunnel in amusement. While these traditions of jokes may seem to be an insignificant, and maybe unnecessary, element of professional sports, it provides a very necessary relief from the stress and pressure that exist in their day-to-day lives. Being able to laugh at themselves and with one another can positively impact both individual and team performance, in addition to improving overall well-being. As a result, it undeniably fuels that purpose that drives our motivation— fun, yourself, and those standing next to you.

That fun and loose mindset can become harder and harder to find as the stakes rise.

Things change as the game evolves from a hobby to a passion and potentially into a career. However, out of all the athletes I have worked with, I can say without a doubt that the ones who laughed the most, especially at themselves, were the ones who achieved the most in their sport—and I don't think it is a coincidence.

When I worked at the sports vision clinic, I frequently worked with Chris Hanson, who was a professional squash player and the back-to-back USA national champion. Chris, who was inducted into the Dartmouth Athletics hall of fame and has had gold medals hanging from his neck, had enough humility and grace (and trust in me) to allow me to throw tennis balls at his face while he was wearing strobe glasses. Strobe glasses are training devices that mimic the effect of strobe lights, blinking on and off and inhibiting the wearer's vision. We would start on the first level, where the glasses blink quickly, and work our way up to the harder settings where the glasses would blink much slower, leaving him in the darkness for longer periods of time. While the goal was for him to be able to catch the balls with limited visual information, there was a lot of failure in the process (and occasionally some face shots that he took in stride).

Chris would always talk throughout our whole session. Usually with me, but sometimes just to himself. Oftentimes it was encouraging and self-motivating, but he never missed an opportunity to include a self-deprecating joke. While it may seem counterintuitive to have external self-talk that can be critical of yourself, the tone and way in which Chris approached his self-criticism was honest enough to promote change but light enough to avoid tension. Chris was one of my favorite clients to work with, not because of the caliber of his achievements and his general motivation and work ethic, but because he had fun with it. Together we were taking on a unique approach to training, which tested the limits of his cognitive and physical ability. It was hard, and I intentionally made it that way. Failure wasn't just a normal part of our process but a majority of it. Every time I planned a session, creating failure was one of my main goals. I was trying to test the limits of not just his cognitive ability but his mental persistence as well. If you couldn't laugh your way through some of those challenges, it would be a very long training session.

I frequently would record some of the drills we did to post on social media, or for my own personal reference when designing training programs in the following weeks. My favorite video I have taken is of Chris. The drill he is doing in the video required an extreme amount of multitasking. You can see him standing about ten yards away from the wall, where there was a grid full of numbers. The grid is similar to one you may see at an eye exam, but all the numbers were the same size. Surrounding the grid were four circular lights set up so they formed a square around the number grid.

Where Chris was standing, there were four dots on the floor: one behind him, one in front of him, and one to each side, each dot a different color. As Chris read the numbers on the grid, the lights flashed one at a time and corresponded with a color of one of the dots on the floor. His job was to use his foot to tap the dot on the floor that matched the color of the light and continue to read the numbers in order. He had to do all this while juggling three tennis balls.

This wasn't meant to be easy. In the video, Chris began the drill and quickly dropped one of the tennis balls. He went to chase the ball as it rolled across the room, and you can hear him mutter under his breath, "Why does this happen to me?" But what you can also hear is him laughing at himself as he picks the ball back up, does a little dance to reset himself, and begins again. And you know what? He dropped the ball again almost instantly. However, after a few minutes, he got it down and was able to work his way through the whole number grid.

It is easy to sell laughter. They say sex sells, but I think laughter sells even more. People will pay time and time again to go see a funny movie or a comedy show. They will repeat activities and go to events that make them laugh with their friends. They will watch the same YouTube or TikTok video over and over again, and they will show it to everyone they know. They will retweet and repost it, contributing to the viral trend and sharing the laugh with not only people they know but also those they don't know. This type of repetitive behavior, of doing the same thing over and over again because it is enjoyable, is also the kind of commitment athletes need in order to find success in their sport. What can keep them coming back to practice every day, running the same drills, perfecting the same routines? For swimmer Missy Franklin, the five-time Olympic gold medalist I mentioned before, a good laugh was an important part of it. In her exclusive letter published by ESPN reflecting on her retirement, she says, "People always ask me when I knew I was good, and I always tell them I truly don't know because all I was concerned with was having fun. I was just being a little girl, spending time with my teammates and closest friends at practice, all while still getting in a good laugh as we gasped for breath at the wall in between intervals."[19] However, while we all know we like to laugh, and that it is innately enjoyable, we don't always understand the value of it. Laughter has so many psychological and physical benefits.

When it comes to physical performance, as I mentioned, laughter automatically relaxes your body. The tension that rests in your shoulders, or your arms, or the pit of your stomach when you are nervous, releases when you laugh, allowing you to execute fine motor skills with fluidity and ease. When your body is physically loose and relaxed, you are also able to play freely and be more mentally in the moment, not getting sucked into the future or stuck too far in the past. You can overcome mistakes more easily, celebrate successes, and enjoy the process each step at a time.

Laughter can even increase your immune system and reduce the physical sensation of pain.[20] Now, most athletes will tell you there is always a little pain somewhere—as we know, you are rarely going to feel 100 percent. But with this knowledge, we may be able to better understand the viral photo of Usain Bolt from the 2016 Olympics in Rio, where he was caught mid-race with a huge smile on his face, while his competition looks more focused and serious. Could his smile, and general joy-filled approach to his craft, be the secret to his success on the track? As his mother said to him in *The Boy Who Learned to Fly*, an animated short created by Gatorade,

"You can always go fast if you keep it light."

Bolt isn't the only one who knows the power of a smile on performance. In the Netflix documentary *Chasing Perfection*, cycling coach Sir Dave Brailsford, who led Great Britain to eight Olympic gold medals at both the 2008 and the 2012 Olympics, discusses how he transformed the British cycling team and nurtured some of the most successful athletes in the UK by focusing not on perfection but on progress. He highlights the little things that impacted their daily approach that he focused on to build momentum in the program. In addition to looking at improvements in their training, nutrition, and equipment, Brailsford asked another important question daily: Are we smiling?

The effects of smiling and laughter have been the subject of scientific research for quite some time, and they were the subject of philosophy before science took hold. Even the Bible says, "A cheerful heart is good medicine, but a crushed spirit dries up the bones," echoing a less modern phrasing of "Laughter is the best medicine."[21] Yet, it still isn't seen as a priority in our lives. Like washing our hands, or taking our vitamins, we don't put laughter on our daily to-do list to stay healthy. We don't make it our goal or intention for our day when we are focused on performing or achieving certain outcomes. However, just because the number of times we laughed isn't always seen as important as the number of miles we ran or how many pounds we were able to squat, I think we should make it our goal—if not for the benefit of our performance, for the benefit of our overall health and quality of life.

So, while we all focus on our goal-setting and choose our short- and long-term goals carefully, I think we would all be missing out on our journey and limiting our potential if we did not emphasize laughter and fun as a part of our goal-setting process. Dr. Colleen Hacker, who has served as the sport psychology consultant for both the USA women's national soccer and hockey teams, even discusses the priority laughter should take in our daily lives with Julie Foudy, former national soccer team player, two-time World Cup champion, and two-time Olympic champion, on Foudy's podcast, appropriately named *Laugher Permitted*. "Mandatory laughter," Dr. Hacker states.[22] "It's not just a frivolous activity; it's not just a frivolous behavior. Yes, it is enjoyable, but it is so much more than that. . . . So, you want to get stronger, laugh more. You want to get healthier, laugh more. The lymphatic system is the highway that clears negative chemicals, buildup, substrates in our body. It is the highway that moves it out. A belly laugh enhances the lymphatic system. Fact, not hypothesis . . . you get a bath of neurochemicals that helps us, an enhanced immune system, and an enhanced lymphatic system. There are medical physicians that prescribe laughter."

This is a game.

While losing is no laughing matter, playing the game always should be.

Results aside, the game should make you smile in between any fits of frustration or disappointing losses. It should make you laugh in between the mistakes you will inevitably make. As quickly as it can build up our hopes and our dreams, yes, this game can break our hearts. But if you don't take it so seriously and you allow yourself to laugh, you will find a persistence, will, and joy that are indestructible.

Lesson 28

CREATE YOUR OWN MOMENTUM

In high school physics, I learned that momentum equals an object's mass times its velocity. A large object moving at an extremely fast pace will have more momentum than a small object moving at a slow pace. Makes sense. When discussing an object's momentum, it is important to realize that the perspective of the observer will influence the evaluation of an object's momentum. Two observers with different frames of reference will interpret an object's momentum very differently. For instance, a person on the sidewalk sees a dog go by in a car. According to that person, that dog had significant momentum. It was moving fast in a particular direction. However, to his owner sitting in the driver's seat beside him, the dog had zero momentum.

Momentum isn't just physical movement, however. There is also psychological momentum, where that perspective or frame of reference is even more important.[23] Psychological momentum has been defined in research as an added or gained psychological power that changes a person's view of themselves and of others. In life and performance, psychological momentum has great potential, but it is perspective that makes it powerful. How you perceive an event will influence the impact that event can have on your momentum, your performance, and ultimately your achievement. While many of us often wait for momentum to occur, true competitors know how to create their own with their thoughts, decisions, and actions.

In sports, momentum doesn't change just the pace of the game but also the competitors' perceptions of one another, instilling the belief in one player that they have an advantage over their opponent. I always found this concept interesting because we think of momentum as this moving physical force, but it is just as much a mental one as a physical one. While an object in motion will stay in motion unless acted on by another force,

the force that can stop it doesn't have to be a brick wall but can be a powerful thought

—one that creates enough friction to slow someone down, or even one that continues to push it forward.

This doesn't mean momentum is invisible to the naked eye. Anyone who has spent enough time watching sports can recognize signs of momentum shifts. You can physically see the confidence grow in one team with their posture and composure, while the other starts to grasp at the air, wondering where their game has gone, feeling hopeless in their pursuit of victory. There is an evident interaction between the physical and mental states at play. The increase in psychological momentum leads to an increase in a competitor's energy, performance levels, self-confidence, and overall effort. As a result, psychological momentum can increase the probability of success.

The early attempts to theoretically understand psychological momentum and demonstrate its influence in sports were in the 1980s, when researchers analyzed the results of racquetball tournaments.[24] It was predicted that in a three-game series, the competitor who won the first game would be more likely to win the second game and therefore the entire series. While winning the first game accounted for half of the necessary games to win, it was also critical in forming the competitors' first impressions of one another's capability. The results in the racquetball games supported the hypothesis of psychological momentum and revealed that early successful performance in the sets gave an advantage to the performer, increasing their chances of winning the series. The authors also highlighted that psychological momentum had a dual effect. Not only did it give an advantage to the competitor who had achieved early success, but it also put the loser at a psychological disadvantage, making the impact of psychological momentum that much more effective.

Research went on to try to replicate these findings in other sports and did so successfully, finding similar results in tennis and even hockey.[25] For instance, scoring the first goal in hockey and outscoring your opponent in the first period increased the probability of winning the game. However, we know the team that scores first doesn't always win. While that first goal sparks the first swing of momentum, numerous momentum shifts can exist within a game and impact the final outcome. As a performer, understanding where that momentum begins and how to manipulate it in your favor can be game changing.

The most comprehensive understanding of momentum looks at the various components within the individual performer that get triggered by the event.[26] This includes an impact on the performer's cognition, affect, physiology, and behavior. If I score first, my thoughts about myself and my ability change, my emotions and feelings of confidence increase, my heart rate and adrenaline boost my motivation, my actions reflect that confidence as I stand taller and hesitate less with the ball, and my overall performance improves. More specifically, these changes happen both in me as the performer and in my opponent. So while my performance is improving, my opponent would experience the opposite effect, including disruptive thoughts, negative emotions, physiological signs of anxiety and stress, behavior that reflects frustration or lack of confidence, and a decrease in their overall performance. As a result, these outcomes continue to compound the effect of the initial momentum swing and influence the overall game.

On January 30, 2009, the headline in the *New Haven Register* read, "Yale Seeks Momentum off Wild Comeback against Colgate."[27] A wild comeback it was. Facing a four-goal deficit to Colgate University with thirteen minutes left in the third period, my dad pulled his goaltender from the net to allow his team an extra skater on the ice. Now, as anyone who has watched any hockey knows, thirteen minutes left is a long time. Pulling your goalie is a strategy that is typically reserved for the final minute or two of the game. Doing it that early is almost unheard of. The decision, however, paid off, and their four-goal deficit suddenly became only three. Reflecting on his successful gamble and the goal it earned them, my dad said, "There was just this feeling on the bench that it could work." With these clear signs of a shift in both cognition and affect, they had a good feeling and belief that they were still in it—the first signs of a momentum shift.

Just over two minutes later, with the goalie back in net, the Yale Bulldogs were up a skater again, this time thanks to a power play. Once again, the Bulldogs capitalized on their opportunity, the score now 4–2. A minute later, a Yale penalty put them on the penalty kill, leaving them a player short and giving Colgate some relief to stop Yale's momentum in its tracks. Ten seconds into the penalty kill, Yale scored again, this time playing a man down. "At that point," my dad was quoted saying, "your players suddenly are not tired anymore." There was an evident physiological shift in his players and their perceived fatigue, and their actions reflected that on the ice. Now only one goal separated them and their opponent. With just under three minutes remaining, Yale was able to tie the game, which they later went on to win one minute into the overtime period. The final score of the wild comeback was 5–4.

Although in retrospect it is easy to credit their win to the gutsy call by my dad behind the bench, some may say he was just lucky he didn't leave his team facing a five-goal deficit. I even remember my dad telling me the next morning that when he walked back onto their bus after the game to head home, the bus driver looked at him, bewildered. "What happened in there?" the bus driver asked. "I was listening on the radio and first they were calling you crazy and then they were calling you a genius." He laughed when he told me the story and agreed he was rolling the dice with his decision. He knew it was a gamble, but it was a gamble he thought was worth taking in order to create some momentum for his players. More importantly, it was an informed gamble he took with clear insight into the players he had on the bench and how to spark a fire within them.

Sports are unpredictable regardless of if you play it safe or take a risk, like the one he took that night. The same two teams can play against each other multiple times and the outcome can vary drastically. In addition, my dad can make the same coaching decision during a different game or with a different team and not be rewarded with the same outcome. In that moment, the decision alone, as crazy as it may have seemed, gave his team confidence and triggered a thought that a comeback was possible. However, for some, the move may have triggered fear and stress. Therefore, having a keen insight into yourself and those on your team is crucial to being able to manage and manipulate those shifts as they occur.

Regardless of the decisions consciously being made on the bench, fluctuations in performance are a natural occurrence in any sporting event. Therefore, athletes and coaches can both benefit from understanding how to maintain or resist these shifts and utilize the phenomenon of momentum to their advantage. This begins with many of the skills we have covered so far in this book: self-talk, emotional management, self-awareness, and focus. If you are able to harness these things, not only will you be able to more effectively resist negative momentum when it pushes you back, but you will also be able to create momentum that propels you forward.

Let's begin with the first two steps in the "momentum chain," the cognitive and affective pieces—your thoughts and emotions. While we all have thoughts and opinions about events as they occur, our perceptions of those events can vary greatly. In order for momentum to have an effect, a performer needs to believe the momentum exists or that the event that happened was strong enough to trigger that momentum. If you have a well-prepared self-talk script, your thoughts will stay on track to keep you focused and maintain a stable belief in your ability, even if something like the other team scoring first happens. Moreover, if you can weather the storm and not get caught in the strong current produced by the emotional ups and downs that occur throughout the competition,

the strongest force will be not the momentum, but you.

The next two steps in the chain are the physiological effect and behavior. While we begin by preparing ourselves to guide our thoughts and embrace our emotions, we know we can't control them. Implementing a breathing technique or another method of manipulating our physiological arousal, whether we need to be settled down or hyped up, is critical. In addition, we have to be deliberate with our behavior, focusing on our body language and the actions we can control. While this physical aspect of momentum is where we can regain some power in response to those moments that can trigger these shifts, our physiology and actions are also where we can start if we want to create our own momentum.

As a coach, my dad made a decision that directly impacted how his team had to play the game. Without a goalie, the adrenaline jumped a bit and they had to adjust their behavior on the ice and focus solely on going to goal and keeping the puck in the offensive zone. They weren't given the option to let down on the ice and fall back defensively. However, the decision you make doesn't have to be so drastic. Simple tactical adjustments can have the same effect. In my graduate school research, one coach discussed how he addressed his team's mindset by changing their strategy on the ice, specifically in the neutral zone, to get his players thinking about moving forward and not playing so defensively. Creating momentum without waiting for an event to trigger it can be as simple as changing your formation or strategy.

For an athlete, the fighter in hockey was known as the ultimate momentum creator, using his actions to increase the arousal in his team and inject some energy into their play. However, fighting isn't the only way to do this. Simply battling hard in the game, standing tall and confidently, communicating with your teammates, and creating opportunities will send the same message. If your opponent is finding success and winning the game, nothing applies more friction to their momentum and their growing confidence than your persistence. Refusing to quit and continuing to play like it is your game to win prevents your opponent from getting comfortable with their lead and can insert just enough doubt into their minds to give you the advantage.

Given the fact that perceived momentum shifts do not always ensure a team victory, it is clear that it is not the sole determinant of performance or outcome. In fact, it is an unreliable factor in sports. Take the game one step at a time.

Momentum shifts feel big and powerful, but they are only as powerful as you make them.

When momentum is working in your favor, feed that fire and let it carry you. If momentum shifts against you, apply friction. Stay focused on the task at hand, and don't get too far ahead of yourself worrying about the result. Momentum will only take you as far as you let it in either direction. Even when he pulled the goalie, my dad admitted that he didn't do it so they could win the game. They were down four goals. He just did it to create some momentum so they could score one goal and start moving in the right direction.

During every competition, there are multiple factors that go into determining who wins. It is not always the strongest or the fastest or the most skilled who comes out victorious. Part of that is due to the psychological factors that play a pivotal role in that unpredictability, and they are a lot less stable than those physical features that athletes train so hard to acquire. These shifts in momentum can make all the difference.

Lesson 29

CHOOSE YOUR TEAM WISELY

As you navigate momentum shifts both in your performance and in life, set goals, and strive to achieve whatever your personal definition of success may be, one of the most influential elements of your experience will be those you surround yourself with—your team. This team includes not just those on the field with you, but those you choose to interact with on a regular basis. While support and encouragement are critical things your team can and should offer you, one of the most overlooked qualities in a teammate is someone who will challenge you.

Those who are willing to be challenged by their teammates are the ones who are most likely to continue to improve rather than plateau in a comfort zone of complacency.

This is the one common thread I have noticed among the most successful people I have ever met. Whether they be an Olympic gold medalist, doctor, lawyer, entrepreneur, parent, or politician, they all have a desire to learn and grow from others. They are the best in their fields, and they never think they have maxed out their knowledge or that they are too far above anyone else to find value in what they could offer them. They fill their bookshelves with never-ending resources and their dinner tables with people who test them and teach them. They reach out to others who can challenge them, by offering new perspective and insight, and help them grow.

Elite athletes, specifically, seek out situations that will make them better. Typically, these situations involve teammates who will help them in that process. Multiple times, I have heard athletes reflect on their decisions about the people they surrounded themselves with, and the ones who achieved greatness deliberately put themselves in situations throughout their lives where they were not the best, but with the people who they believed would make them better. Former NFL wide receiver Julian Edelman, for instance, moved out to California in the off-season just so he could be near Tom Brady and possibly train with him. Although Brady only called him twice the first year, eventually it became a consistent part of both of their off-season schedules. While Edelman has been quoted saying that Brady "singlehandedly helped me, just by letting me be around him in the offseason, develop my game and see what it took to become a professional on and off the field," Edelman really helped himself the most by choosing to surround himself with the right people who could teach him and help him grow.[28]

Coaches may not need to be pushed physically, but they can still find value in having a team that challenges them to improve. My research in graduate school reflected this, as many of the coaches I spoke to referenced their assistant coaches and staff as being valuable resources for them. The coaches relied on their input and their insight to make decisions, and more importantly, they hired people they knew would make them better coaches. The most successful coaches didn't want an assistant who would blindly accept and agree with everything they said, but someone who would challenge them and make sure collectively they made the best possible decisions for the team. I smiled as I gathered this data because it sounded all too familiar to me.

When Yale won their national championship in 2013, my dad had Red Gendron on the bench beside him. Red didn't exactly have the resume that reflected a typical assistant coach at the collegiate level. In fact, by most standards, he was overqualified. With over thirty years of coaching experience under his belt, Red already had an NCAA championship and two Stanley Cup rings before he took the job at Yale. He had started his career in the early eighties as a history teacher and coach in Vermont, where he won four state titles, and that educational spirit never left him. In his role as a coach, he taught his players countless life lessons with some hockey skills mixed in. As he has been quoted saying numerous times, "My job is that when you leave college you are not only a better hockey player but also a great person."

When discussing his coaching legacy, people often refer to Red as a teacher first and foremost, and my dad, although the head coach, was very much a willing student of Red's. After Red unexpectedly passed away in the spring of 2021 from a heart attack, my dad reflected on their time together behind the bench. I recall him telling me how Red made him better and how much he learned from him. Red wouldn't let my dad make a decision without challenging him on it to make sure he had considered all angles and possibilities. Both men who had achieved significant success in their careers were eager to get better and learn from each other. Furthermore, they were both greatly impacted by Dan Muse, my dad's other assistant, who challenged them to think like a younger coach. He brought in a different perspective and angle that pushed the two veteran coaches to improve, and as a team, they all got better.

In my own life, people have frequently pointed out that

I tend to find myself in a school setting year after year. It is clear that I value learning as a lifelong endeavor. However, as people explain that I am always either a student or a teacher somewhere, what they don't realize is that I am only sometimes the teacher, but I am always, always a student. I have learned more standing at the front of my classroom than I ever did when I was sitting behind a desk, the same way that I have learned more standing on the sideline as a coach than I did when I was playing on the field. I love teaching people new skills and helping them find new insight and perspectives, but I love that I can keep learning from them even more. Therefore, in order to keep learning, I make a point to continue to surround myself with people who can keep teaching me new things.

I have coached alone before, I have been the only psychology teacher at my school, and I have run a business independently. While I take great pride in the accomplishments that I was able to have in those solo endeavors, I quickly realized how limited my growth was on my own. In order to reach my full potential, I needed people around me to help me get there. The impact that others have had on me isn't always determined by expertise or age, but by differing opinions, experiences, and ideas. For instance, as a teacher and coach, I am always in awe of the curiosity that exists in the minds of my students and athletes. They frequently ask questions, challenge me, and force me to become better and smarter at my job every day. They are all some of the most valuable members of my team.

More importantly, I think the willingness and desire to learn is one of the most important examples you can set as a coach. When I first began teaching and coaching, I felt extremely unprepared and underqualified, and those questions my kids would ask terrified me. I might not know the answer, I worried, as someone raised their hand with a question. At first, I thought it was terrible to approach my job with such self-doubt and insecurity. However, with more experience, I feel much more prepared, but I also have just grown more comfortable with the uncertainty. I know much more now than I did when I started, but there is still so much I am able to learn every day, and I think my willingness and desire to learn is my greatest strength. As coaches, parents, and teachers, we always want to model the behavior we hope to foster in those we are leading. Model good sportsmanship, respect and kindness, and good manners. However, sometimes we get so caught up in the role or title of coach, teacher, or adult that we don't model some of the most important behaviors, like learning and growing. None of us are finished products, and if I am able to embrace the learning process in front of my student athletes by asking questions just as much as I answer them, then I am both giving and getting more out of those relationships than if I simply tried to bestow information.

Whether it's your own students, your players, your coaches, your teammates, your family, or anyone else, we can all learn from those around us. Even NFL coach Bill Belichick, who began his coaching career in 1975, is still learning from his players. In the fall of 2021, Belichick spoke about one player in particular, New England Patriots kicker Nick Folk. "He's helpful, and very, very knowledgeable," Belichick claimed.[29] "I've learned a lot from Nick Folk. I'll say that. I've learned a lot. He's really taught me a lot of little things that honestly, I hadn't really thought that much about, and once he pointed them out, I was kind of disappointed in myself that I didn't put a little more importance on it earlier."

Improving yourself and achieving success isn't a solo endeavor.

We all need a team to help us along the way. It can help and provide guidance during adversity, comfort us when we need support, celebrate us when we sometimes forget to, and, most importantly, teach us the lessons we wouldn't have discovered on our own. While many of our teammates may be selected for us, we all have the power to reach out to others, connect with people, and grow our team. The people we choose to surround ourselves with will be one of the most valuable decisions we can make. Find people who push you, who test you, who challenge you, but, most importantly, who love you, and you will already have found success.

[THE FINAL LESSON]

Lesson 30

SPORTS AREN'T EVERYTHING

Growing up around sports, playing them, and now working with them, I have learned a lot from these games. However, the most important lesson I have taken away from these experiences is that sports aren't everything. They may be something you do. They may even be something you love and make a living from, but it is the things the games give you that matter the most, not the games themselves—the lessons they teach you, the experiences they provide you, and, most importantly, the people they bond you to. Every single person I ever met who competed at the highest level, I always knew as someone's father, mother, brother, sister, son, or daughter first. That never changed, regardless of the outcome of the game or even if the game was no longer there anymore. In fact, it is when the sports don't go well that those other identities become stronger and matter more.

Sure, winning is fun, and being able to share that with the people you love is incredible. It is also amazing to see everyone who shows up to a championship parade after a team wins. But have you ever waited with the families after losing it all? I have, many times. Because only one team wins the championship. Only one team gets to take a champagne shower while their opponents stand under hot running water, sometimes until it turns cold, watching it slip through their fingers. Once they've dried off, they go see the people who were willing to wait hours after the game for a five-second hug, those who applaud their efforts, not out of pity but out of genuine love and true pride.

In 2018, the Olympics were in South Korea, and for the first time since 1994, NHL players were not allowed to compete. This meant the USA roster was made up of college players, ex-NHL players, and everything in between (barring anyone with an NHL contract). Ages on their roster ranged from twenty to thirty-nine years old. A week before their first game, they flew in from all over the world. A week before their first game, at the Olympics, they had their first official practice all together. Despite the numerous challenges the team had coming into the Olympics, they quickly became a team and competed better and better in each opportunity they had.

Unfortunately, their tournament was cut short in the quarterfinals, in a shootout against the Czech Republic. Team USA's Olympic journey was over. Now, I could write about the crossbar Brian O'Neill hit with two minutes remaining in the game. Or I could describe the feeling of confidence that was building not only in the players on the ice but also in their supporters in the crowd as overtime continued on. Just a few more minutes of playing, we all thought. Just another shift, maybe. One more chance. Team USA had a goal coming, we could all feel it. Except the clock ran out before that goal could come. But that's not what this story is about. No, the story is about the group of people, waiting on the concourse for their fathers, sons, and brothers.

There was no family room or waiting area at the arena in Gangneung like we were accustomed to back home. There was nowhere for us to go once the game ended. So, we just stayed where we were, right there on the concourse between concession stands selling ddukbokki (some form of spicy rice cakes) and nachos (without cheese or salsa, so essentially chips). Olympic personnel shuffled people around us and out the door, encouraging us to leave as well. But we waited. Not for a celebration, or a medal moment, or an autograph. Just for the people we loved. The rink emptied out around us, and as time continued to pass, you could see the nervous faces of those working in the rink as the language barrier made their efforts to get us to leave even more futile than if we had understood them completely. Eventually, someone came with a megaphone and in English told us to leave. In the most American fashion, we stayed put. Finally, the team came out and we were able to give our hugs and say our brief hellos and goodbyes before security came to escort us out of the rink.

It has never been about winning. We love to do it. We would prefer to if given the choice, but it isn't about that. It has never even been about the sport, but more about what the sport has given us. Yes, it has given us plenty of heartbreak and tears, disappointments that take lifetimes to forget. But it also has given us an extended family and ten lifetimes' worth of experiences. It has brought us places we would have never gone to, but more importantly it also always brings us home. There have been times in my life when my family has been all over the map, spread out across different countries and even time zones. But on a Friday night during the winter season, we all connect over a game. If we can't physically be there, we mentally are—a good-luck text before, a postgame recap after.

Because of my life, I relate a lot of things to sports. The lessons in this book are geared toward athletes and coaches, but they can be applied to anyone. The playing field is just my chosen classroom because it is an area that makes the most sense to me, especially in times when life feels like it isn't making any sense. Sports have helped me construct clearer perspectives about the world around me, and whether you are an athlete competing in a rec league or at the professional level, or have never picked up any ball in your life, we are all competing and performing. We are all playing the same game that life has presented us with. We are all both coaches and players in our own games. We are calling the plays, taking the shots, making the save. Sometimes we can recruit other people to be on our team for a particular game or season. Sometimes our individual games can coexist alongside each other, but sometimes our games overlap, and for me to score to get a win means you're going to lose. But we are all playing the game. Some of us train harder than others, some of us play a smart game, some play dirty, some are skilled but lazy.

But there is one consistent truth, and that is that the game can suck. It can test you, challenge you, and let you down. And no matter how many rules or referees you have, sometimes it just doesn't seem fair. Sometimes you'll do everything you can, and you'll still lose. Sometimes you watch someone else win your trophy, score your goal, and steal your dream. But the worst thing?

The worst is when we take ourselves out of our own game simply because it isn't going how we wanted or expected it to.

Sports have given me so much in my life; I wouldn't even know where to begin to truly acknowledge it all. But more importantly, I've realized I can't eliminate it from my story. When I stopped playing soccer, I realized I couldn't simply walk away because there was too much value for me in the game. Even to this day, there are too many lessons I still haven't learned and too many mistakes I still haven't made. I like to think there are also plenty of successes I have yet to earn and experience, but to be honest, even if I never won another game, I'd still stick around. The scoreboards, the games, the sports themselves aren't everything. There's a lot more to this life, but for me, sports add value to my life that I wouldn't want to miss out on. They make my friendships stronger, they make my family closer, and they've made me a lot better of a person. And for that I am forever grateful and indebted to them.

Notes

Part One

[1] Henrik Gustafsson, Guillaume Martinent, Sandrine Isoard-Gautheur, Peter Hassmén, and Emma Guillet-Descas, "Performance Based Self-Esteem and Athlete-Identity in Athlete Burnout: A Person-Centered Approach," *Psychology of Sport and Exercise* 38 (September 2018): 56–60, https://www.sciencedirect.com/science/article/abs/pii/S146902921730818X.

[2] Patrick L. Hill, Nancy L. Sin, Nicholas A. Turiano, Anthony L. Burrow, and David M. Almeida, "Sense of Purpose Moderates the Associations Between Daily Stressors and Daily Well-Being," *Annals of Behavioral Medicine* 52, no. 8 (August 2018): 724–29, http://midus.wisc.edu/findings/pdfs/1762.pdf.

[3] Áine Cain, "Brothers Share What It Was Like Quitting Their Corporate Jobs to Sell Ties on the Beach and Cofound Vineyard Vines, a Company Worth Nearly $1 Billion," Business Insider, September 28, 2016, https://www.businessinsider.com/brothers-who-founded-vineyard-vines-reveal-why-they-quit-their-jobs-2016-9.

[4] Robert Weinberg, Dave Yukelson, Damon Burton, and Daniel Weigand, "Perceived Goal Setting Practices of Olympic Athletes: An Exploratory Investigation," *Sport Psychologist* 14, no. 3 (September 2000): 279–95, https://doi.org/10.1123/tsp.14.3.279.

[5] PGA Tour, Twitter post, June 13th 2020, 11:20 a.m., https://twitter.com/PGATOUR/status/1271824787921350656.

[6] John T. Cacioppo, Stephanie Cacioppo, and Dorret I. Boomsma, "Evolutionary Mechanisms for Loneliness," *Cognition and Emotion* 28, no. 1 (2014): 3–21, https://doi.org/ 10.1080/02699931.2013.837379.

7 Abby Wambach, *Wolfpack: How to Come Together, Unleash Our Power, and Change the Game* (New York: Celadon Books, 2019).

8 Aspen Project Play, "Survey: Kids Quit Most Sports By Age 11," August 1, 2019, https://www.aspenprojectplay.org/national-youth-sport-survey/kids-quit-most-sports-by-age-11.

9 Jeff R. Crane and Viviene A. Temple, "A Systematic Review of Dropout from Organized Sport among Children and Youth," *European Physical Education Review* 21, no. 1 (January 2014): 114–31, researchgate.net/publication/273289197_A_systematic_review_of_dropout_from_organized_sport_among_children_and_youth.

10 Cristina Corbin, "Experts Cite 'Bully Parents' in Decline in Youth Sports Participation Nationwide," May 31, 2019, https://www.foxnews.com/sports/experts-cite-bully-parents-in-decline-in-youth-sports-participation.

11 Peter Gröpel, Christopher Mesagno, and Jürgen Beckmann, "Pre-Shot Routines to Improve Competition Performance: A Case Study of a Group of Elite Pistol Shooters," *Case Studies in Sport and Exercise Psychology* 4, no. 1 (March 2020), https://doi.org/10.1123/cssep.2019-0039.

12 Michael Farber, "The Crosby Conundrum: Entering Middle Age, Who Is Sid the Kid?" *Sports Illustrated*, February 26, 2016, https://www.si.com/nhl/2016/03/03/sidney-crosby-sports-illustrated-crosby-conundrum-michael-farber.

13 Sean Leahy, "Marc-Andre Fleury, Matt Murray and Their Lasting Friendship Formed in Pittsburgh," NBC Sports, December 14, 2017, https://nhl.nbcsports.com/2017/12/14/marc-andre-fleury-matt-murray-and-their-lasting-friendship-formed-in-pittsburgh/.

14 Brock Bastian, Jolanda Jetten, and Laura J. Ferris, "Pain as Social Glue: Shared Pain Increases Cooperation," *Psychological Science* 25, no. 11 (September 2014): 2079–85, https://journals.sagepub.com/doi/abs/10.1177/0956797614545886.

15 Jennifer Calfas, "Desiree Linden Just Became the First American Woman to Win the Boston Marathon in Three Decades," *Time*, April 16, 2018, https://time.com/5241721/desiree-linden-boston-marathon-2018/.

16 "Des Linden + Brooks: Keep Showing Up," YouTube, March 3, 2019, https://www.youtube.com/watch?v=KgLcD7pLrvY.

[17] Tim O'Shei, "Is Dahlin the Sabres' Savior? The Psychology of First-Round Hype," *Buffalo News*, June 21, 2018, https://buffalonews.com/sports/bills/is-dahlin-the-sabres-savior-the-psychology-of-first-round-hype/article_9039359f-9a14-5ff8-9255-2ebdc561f07c.html.

[18] Cork Gaines, "15-Year-Old Cori Gauff Used an Underdog Mental [19] Trick Made Famous by the Movie 'Hoosiers' to Upset Venus Williams at Wimbledon," Business Insider, July 1, 2019, https://www.businessinsider.com/cori-coco-gauff-upset-venus-williams-hoosiers-2019-7.

[19] Mark Tallentire, "Pragmatic Rory McIlroy Plays Open Conditions to Stay in Contention," *Guardian*, July 20, 2018, https://www.theguardian.com/sport/2018/jul/20/pragmatic-rory-mcilroy-plays-conditions-stay-contention.

[20] Jennifer Krizman, Tory Lindley, Silvia Bonacina, Danielle Colegrove, Travis White-Schwoch, and Nina Kraus, "Play Sports for a Quieter Brain: Evidence from Division I Collegiate Athletes," *Sports Health: A Multidisciplinary Approach* 12, no. 2 (2020): 154–58, https://journals.sagepub.com/doi/10.1177/1941738119892275.

[21] Ben Morse, "Gold Medal-Winning Athletes Swerve Social Media to Avoid 'External Pressure,'" CNN, July 28, 2021, https://www.cnn.com/2021/07/28/sport/ariarne-titmus-annemiek-van-vleuten-social-media-mental-health-simone-biles-tokyo-2020-spt-intl/index.html.

[22] Associated Press, "Team USA Gymnast Suni Lee 'Probably Going to Delete Twitter' after Bronze Medal," *Sports Illustrated*, August 3, 2021, https://www.si.com/olympics/2021/08/03/suni-lee-olympics-bronze-medal-delete-twitter.

Part Two

[1] James Phillips, "He's Human! Lionel Messi Is Sick Due to Nerves, Reveals Argentina Boss Alejandro Sabella," *Metro*, June 10, 2014, https://metro.co.uk/2014/06/10/hes-human-lionel-messi-is-sick-due-to-nerves-reveals-argentina-boss-alejandro-sabella-4757070/.

[2] Jack Barbalet, "Emotion," *Contexts* 5, no. 2 (May 2006): 51–53, https://doi.org/10.1525/ctx.2006.5.2.51.

[3] Alex Davidow, "John Tortorella and the 7 Angriest Coaches in the NHL Right Now," Bleacher Report, June 5, 2012, https://bleacher-report.com/articles/1208296-john-tortorella-and-the-7-angriest-coaches-in-the-nhl-right-now.

[4] Martin Fennelly, "With Johnny Torts in Town, It's All Over but the Shouting," *Tampa Bay Times*, April 10, 2019, https://www.tampabay.com/sports/2019/04/10/with-johnny-torts-in-town-its-all-over-but-the-shouting/.

[5] Antonio Damasio, *Descartes' Error: Emotion, Reason, and the Human Brain* (New York: Penguin, 2005).

[6] Daniel Goleman, *The Brain and Emotional Intelligence: New Insights* (Florence, MA: More Than Sound, 2011).

[7] Sam Smith, "Michael Jordan Makes a Hall of Fame Address," Chicago Bulls. NBA.com/bulls, September 12, 2009. https://www.nba.com/bulls/news/jordanhof_speech_090912.html.

[8] Goleman, *The Brain and Emotional Intelligence.*

[9] Philip Ulrich and Susan K. Lutgendorf, "Journaling about Stressful Events: Effects of Cognitive Processing and Emotional Expression," *Annals of Behavioral Medicine* 24, no. 3 (2002): 244–50, http://transformationalchange.pbworks.com/f/stressjournaling.pdf.

[10] Daniel J. Siegel, *Mindsight: The New Science of Personal Transformation* (New York: Bantam, 2010).

[11] Lori A. Zoellner, Jonathan S. Abramowitz, and Sally A. Moore, "Flooding," in *Cognitive Behavior Therapy*, ed. William O'Donohue, Jane E. Fisher, and Steven C. Hayes (Hoboken: John Wiley & Sons, 2003), 160.

[12] David A. Oakley and Peter W. Halligan, "What If Consciousness Is Not What Drives the Human Mind?" The Conversation, November 22, 2017, https://theconversation.com/what-if-consciousness-is-not-what-drives-the-human-mind-86785; David A. Oakley and Peter W. Halligan, "Chasing the Rainbow: The Nonconscious Nature of Being," *Frontiers in Psychology*, November 14, 2017, https://doi.org/10.3389/fpsyg.2017.01924.

[13] Shauna L. Shapiro, Linda E. Carlson, John A. Astin, and Benedict Freedman, "Mechanisms of Mindfulness," *Journal of Clinical Psychology* 62, no. 3 (March 2006): 373–86, https://doi.org/10.1002/jclp.20237.

[14] Amy Cuddy, *Presence: Bringing Your Boldest Self to Your Biggest Challenges* (New York: Little, Brown, 2015).

[15] NFL Films "Adrian Peterson, Emmanuel Sanders & MORE Stars Mic'd Up Self Talk," YouTube, March 2, 2016, https://www.youtube.com/watch?v=BRJLfTIPpBE.

[16] Sam Weinman, *Win At Losing: How Our Biggest Setbacks Can Lead to Our Greatest Gains* (New York: Penguin Random House, 2016).

[17] Timothy Gallwey, *The Inner Game of Tennis* (New York, Bantam Books, 1979).

[18] "A willful and deliberate focus on all that is good in one's life will shift one's baseline temperament and increase feelings of well-being. But it requires a decision, and it requires practice." John D. Kelly, IV, "Your Best Life: Breaking the Cycle: The Power of Gratitude," *Clinical Orthopaedics and Related Research* 474, no. 12 (December 2016): 2594–97, https://www.ncbi.nlm.nih.gov/pmc/articles/PMC5085955/.

[19] Jane Taylor Wilson, "Brightening the Mind: The Impact of Practicing Gratitude on Focus and Resilience in Learning," *Journal of the Scholarship of Teaching and Learning* 16, no. 4 (August 2016): 1–13, https://files.eric.ed.gov/fulltext/EJ1112485.pdf.

[20] Nicole T. Gabana, Jesse Steinfeldt, Y. Joel Wong, Y. Barry Chung, and Dubravka Svetina, "Attitude of Gratitude: Exploring the Implementation of a Gratitude Intervention with College Athletes," *Journal of Applied Sport Psychology* 31, no. 3 (2019): 273–84, https://doi.org/10.1080/10413200.2018.1498956.

[21] Julia Allain, Gordon A. Bloom, and Wade D. Gilbert, "Successful High-Performance Ice Hockey Coaches' Intermission Routines and Situational Factors That Guide Implementation," *Sport Psychologist* 32, no. 3 (2018): 210–19, https://doi.org/10.1123/tsp.2017-0088.

[22] Daniel Goleman and Richard E. Boyatzis, "Social Intelligence and the Biology of Leadership," *Harvard Business Review*, September 2008, https://hbr.org/2008/09/social-intelligence-and-the-biology-of-leadership; Marie T. Dasborough, "Cognitive Asymmetry in Employee Emotional Reactions to Leadership Behaviors," *Leadership Quarterly* 17, no. 2 (April 2006): 163–78, https://doi.org/10.1016/j.leaqua.2005.12.004.

[23] Goleman, *The Brain and Emotional Intelligence.*

[24] "Zen Principles Phil Jackson Used to Coach Dennis Rodman | SuperSoul Sunday | Oprah Winfrey Network," YouTube, https://www.youtube.com/watch?v=vKAEH_L-v98.

[25] L. J. Fallowfield, V. A. Jenkins, and H. A. Beveridge, "Truth May Hurt But Deceit Hurts More: Communication in Palliative Care," *Palliative Medicine* 16, no. 4 (2002): 297–303, https://citeseerx.ist.psu.edu/viewdoc/download?doi=10.1.1.993.3692&rep=rep1&type=pdf.

[26] Carol Dweck, *Mindset: The New Psychology of Success* (New York: Ballantine Books, 2006).

[27] Kim Encel, Christopher Mesagno, and Helen Brown, "Facebook Use and Its Relationship with Sport Anxiety," *Journal of Sports Sciences* 35, no. 8 (April 2017): 756–61, https://doi.org/10.1080/02640414.2016.1186817.

[28] International Olympic Committee (IOC), *Handbook of Sports Medicine and Science: Sport Psychology*, ed. Britton W. Brewer (West Sussex: Wiley-Blackwell, 2009).

[29] Fennelly, "With Johnny Torts in Town."

[30] IOC, *Handbook of Sports Medicine and Science.*

[31] L. F. Cummins, M. R. Nadorff, and A. E. Kelly, "Winning and Positive Affect Can Lead to Reckless Gambling," *Psychology of Addictive Behaviors* 23, no. 2 (2009): 287–94, https://doi.org/10.1037/a0014783.

[32] Weinman, *Win at Losing.*

Part Three

[1] "Super Bowl MVP Nick Foles Shares Awesome Advice About Failure In Life," YouTube, February 7, 2018, https://www.youtube.com/watch?v=TVdYAyNLG_8.

[2] "What We Learned from Wednesday's Media Availability." Kansas City Chiefs, August 1, 2018. https://www.chiefs.com/news/what-we-learned-from-wednesday-s-media-availability-2.

[3] Janet Metcalfe, "Learning from Errors," *Annual Review of Psychology* 68 (January 2017): 465–89, https://www.annualreviews.org/doi/abs/10.1146/annurev-psych-010416-044022.

[4] Faieza Chowdhury, "Grade Inflation: Causes, Consequences, and Cure," *Journal of Education and Learning* 7, no. 6 (2018), https://files.eric.ed.gov/fulltext/EJ1191199.pdf.

[5] Sally Jenkins, "The Secret to Buzzer-Beaters? It's All in the (Mental) Release," *Washington Post*, March 22, 2018, https://www.chicagotribune.com/sports/college/ct-spt-ncaa-tournament-buzzer-beaters-20180322-story.html.

[6] Fred C. Lunenburg, "Goal-Setting Theory of Motivation," *International Journal of Management, Business, and Administration* 15, no. 1 (2011), http://nationalforum.com/Electronic%20Journal%20Volumes/Lunenburg,%20Fred%20C.%20Goal-Setting%20Theoryof%20Motivation%20IJMBA%20V15%20N1%202011.pdf.

[7] Megan Sauer, "Bradie Tennell's Secret to Consistency," U.S. Figure Skating Fan Zone, https://usfigureskatingfanzone.com/news/2020/12/9/rinkside-bradie-tennells-secret-to-consistency.aspx.

[8] Johnny Damon, "Letter to My Younger Self," *Players' Tribune*, October 4, 2018, https://www.theplayerstribune.com/articles/johnny-damon-baseball-letter-to-my-younger-self.

[9] Missy Franklin, "Episode 51: Missy Franklin," December 9, 2020, in Laughter Permitted with Julie Foudy, podcast.

[10] Adam Oates, "Spittin' Chiclets Episode 115: Featuring Adam Oates," October 11, 2018, in Spittin' Chiclets, podcast.

[11] Daniel Avrahami, Kristin Williams, Matthew L. Lee, Nami Tokunaga, Yulius Tjahjadi, and Jennifer Marlow, "Celebrating Everyday Success: Improving Engagement and Motivation Using a System for Recording Daily Highlights," CHI '20: Proceedings of the 2020 CHI Conference on Human Factors in Computing Systems (April 2020): 1–13, https://doi.org/10.1145/3313831.3376369.

[12] Don Yaeger, "Four Ways to Be Great and Celebrate: Lessons from Chicago Cub David Bote," *Forbes*, August 22, 2018, https://www.forbes.com/sites/donyaeger/2018/08/22/four-ways-to-be-great-and-celebrate-lessons-from-chicago-cub-david-bote/?sh=5c8878c31eb9.

[13] Nguyen, Kevin. "Naomi Osaka Is the Coolest Thing in Tennis," *GQ*, May 24, 2018. https://www.gq.com/story/naomi-osaka-is-the-coolest-thing-in-tennis.

[14] "There's Zero Fear in His Game: Jack Hughes Revels in Chance to Play on Big Stage," YouTube, January 4, 2019, https://www.youtube.com/watch?v=DM0q6RkK_MU.

[15] Karen Crouse, "Katie Ledecky Crosses into the World of Pro Sports: It Feels Like Home," *New York Times*, August 9, 2018, https://www.nytimes.com/2018/08/09/sports/katie-ledecky-swimming.html.

[16] Weinberg, Robert S. n.d. "Goal Setting in Sport and Exercise: Research to Practice," *Exploring Sport and Exercise Psychology* (2nd Ed.), 25–48, https://doi.org/10.1037/10465-003.

[17] Robert S. Rubin, "Will the Real SMART Goals Please Stand Up?" January 2002, https://citeseerx.ist.psu.edu/viewdoc/download?doi=10.1.1.523.6999&rep=rep1&type=pdf.

[18] JongEun Kim, "Therapeutic Benefits of Laughter in Mental Health: A Theoretical Review," *Tohoku Journal of Experimental Medicine* 239 no. 3 (July 2016): 243–49, https://www.jstage.jst.go.jp/article/tjem/239/3/239_243/_pdf.

[19] Missy Franklin, "It Took Me a Long Time to Say 'I Am Retiring,' but Now I'm Ready," ESPN, December 18, 2018, https://www.espn.com/espnw/voices/story/_/id/25568406/missy-franklin-explains-why-now-time-retire-competitive-swimming.

[20] Margaret Stuber, Sherry Dunay Hilber, Lisa Libman Mintzer, Marleen Castaneda, Dorie Glover, and Lonnie Zeltzer, "Laughter, Humor and Pain Perception in Children: A Pilot Study," *Evidence-Based Complementary and Alternative Medicine* 6 (2009): 457626, https://www.hindawi.com/journals/ecam/2009/457626/; R. I. M. Dunbar, Rebecca Baron, Anna Frangou, Eiluned Pearce, Edwin J. C. van Leeuwen, Julie Stow, Giselle Partridge, Ian MacDonald, Vincent Barra, and Mark van Vugt, "Social Laughter Is Correlated with an Elevated Pain Threshold," *Proceedings of the Royal Society* B 279, no. 1731 (March 2012), https://doi.org/10.1098/rspb.2011.1373.

[21] Proverbs 17:22.

[22] "Episode 31: Dr. Colleen Hacker," March 18, 2020, in Laughter Permitted with Julie Foudy, podcast.

[23] Seppo Iso-Ahola and Ken Mobily, "'Psychological Momentum': A Phenomenon and an Empirical (Unobtrusive) Validation of Its Influence in a Competitive Sport Tournament," *Psychological Reports* 46, no. 2 (April 1980): 391–401.

[24] Seppo Iso-Ahola, and W. J. Blanchard, "Psychological Momentum and Competitive Sport Performance: A Field Study," *Perceptual and Motor Skills* 62, no. 3 (1986): 763–68; Iso-Ahola and Mobily, "'Psychological Momentum,'" 391–401.

[25] William F. Gayton, Michael Very, and Joseph Hearns, "Psychological Momentum in Team Sports," *Journal of Sport Behavior* 16, no. 3 (1993): 121–23; Peggy A. Richardson, William Adler, and Douglas Hankes, "Game, Set, Match: Psychological Momentum in Tennis," *Sport Psychologist* 2, no. 1 (1988): 69–76; John M. Silva, Charles J. Hardy, and R. Kelly Crace, "Analysis of Psychological Momentum in Intercollegiate Tennis," *Journal of Sport and Exercise Psychology* 10, no. 3 (1988): 346–54.

[26] Jim Taylor and Andrew Demick, "A Multidimensional Model of Momentum in Sports," Journal of Applied Sport Psychology 6, no. 1 (1994): 51–70.

[27] Malafronte, Chip. "Yale Seeks Momentum off Wild Comeback against Colgate," *New Haven Register,* January 30, 2009, https://www.nhregister.com/news/article/Yale-seeks-momentum-off-wild-comeback-against-11620660.php.

[28] Michael Hurley, "Unsurprisingly, Julian Edelman Had a Lot to Say About Tom Brady after QB's Retirement," CBS Boston, February 2, 2022, https://boston.cbslocal.com/2022/02/02/julian-edelman-has-a-lot-to-say-tom-brady-retirement/.

[29] Chris Mason, "Patriots' Bill Belichick: 'I've Learned a Lot from Nick Folk,' Says Kicker Taught 'Little Things' He'd Never Noticed," Mass Live, November 26, 2021, https://www.masslive.com/patriots/2021/11/patriots-bill-belichick-ive-learned-a-lot-from-nick-folk-says-kicker-taught-little-things-hed-never-noticed.html.

Acknowledgments

"Whatever you do in life, surround yourself with smart people who'll argue with you."

—John Wooden

First and foremost, I want to thank everyone who inspired and influenced these lessons. This book would not exist if it weren't for the many people in my life that I have been fortunate enough to learn from both directly and indirectly. Everyone mentioned in these pages has played a significant role in shaping my perspective on life and helped me formulate these lessons, whether they know it or not. In a way, these pages are written by them as much as they are written by me. I also want to thank my family, who read countless drafts, responded to constant text messages, and engaged in endless conversations about every tiny step in this process. And finally, the biggest thank you goes to the MVP, Victoria Petelin. You not only saw the potential in my disorganized thoughts and ideas but also stuck with me through the roughest of drafts, challenged me to be better, and guided me to the finish line. I used to think writing was a solo endeavor, but you made me realize it is just as much of a team sport as anything else I have ever participated in, and I couldn't have been more fortunate to have you on my team!

About the Author

Julia Allain is a sport psychology consultant and mental skills coach. As the founder of Allain Mental Performance LLC, she has worked with numerous collegiate, professional, and internationally competitive athletes, including USA Hockey's National Team Development Program. Allain earned her master's degree in sport psychology from McGill University, where her research was published in *The Sport Psychologist*. She has also taught psychology and coached at various private schools. For more information about speaking engagements or consulting work please visit www.AllainMentalPerformance.com.